WISDOM OF THE
PEACEFUL WARRIOR

Books by Dan Millman

The Peaceful Warrior Saga

Way of the Peaceful Warrior
Sacred Journey of the Peaceful Warrior
The Journeys of Socrates

Guidebooks

The Life You Were Born to Live
Everyday Enlightenment
No Ordinary Moments
Living on Purpose
The Laws of Spirit
Body Mind Mastery

For Children

Secret of the Peaceful Warrior
Quest for the Crystal Castle

For more information about Dan Millman's work:
www.peacefulwarrior.com

WISDOM OF THE
PEACEFUL WARRIOR

A COMPANION TO
THE BOOK THAT CHANGES LIVES

DAN MILLMAN

H J KRAMER

published in a joint venture with

NEW WORLD LIBRARY
NOVATO, CALIFORNIA

An H J Kramer Book
published in a joint venture with
New World Library

Editorial office: Administrative office:
H J Kramer Inc.   New World Library
P.O. Box 1082   14 Pamaron Way
Tiburon, California 94920   Novato, California 94949

Edited by Nancy Grimley Carleton
Text design and typography by Tona Pearce Myers

Library of Congress Cataloging-in-Publication Data
Millman, Dan.
Wisdom of the peaceful warrior : a companion to the book that changes lives / Dan Millman.
    p.   cm.
ISBN-13: 978-1-932073-21-8 (pbk. : alk. paper)
1. Spiritual life. I. Title.
BL624.M534 2006
204'.4—dc22   2006025569

First printing, February 2007
ISBN 978-1-932073-21-8
Printed in Canada on acid-free paper

10   9   8   7   6

To all those exploring the depths of life,
passing through the dark night,
drawn by the light.

Wisdom begins in wonder.

— SOCRATES (470–399 BCE)

CONTENTS

On Book Two: The Warrior's Training

On Book Three: Unreasonable Happiness

INTRODUCTION

COMMENTARIES
TO LIGHT THE WAY

To the illumined mind the whole world
burns and sparkles with light.

—— RALPH WALDO EMERSON

What if, on a spring day in 2006, moved by a sudden sense of nostalgia, I had driven back to Berkeley and was walking alone through Tilden Park when, to my complete astonishment, out of the shadows stepped my old mentor, Socrates, not looking a day older than when we had parted.

And suppose he had held up a copy of *Way of the Peaceful Warrior* and said, "You got a lot of things right, Dan, but you left some points out of focus. Sit down — I'm going to explain a few things you didn't quite grasp."

He would have been right, as usual. After all, I could only hear and remember and relate what I'd learned from my then-current state of awareness.

Now, more than forty years have passed since our first meeting on a starry winter's night in 1966. It wasn't until 1980, fourteen years later, that I wrote *Way of the Peaceful Warrior*, relating the experiences and lessons that followed. Many of the incidents in the book occurred just as I described them; others did not. Yet the teachings remain as true as they are timeless.

The wisdom in *Way of the Peaceful Warrior* is not mine or even that of Socrates; it belong to all of us. Such principles and perspectives were expressed long ago in the Analects of Confucius, the writings of Plato and Aristotle, and the teachings of Jesus, Buddha, Muhammad, Lao Tzu, Chuang Tzu, Hillel, and others. But few of us are likely to explore all the ancient texts, which is why each new generation needs fresh voices to remind us of our global heritage of wisdom, in a language appropriate to each era and culture. I am but one of many such voices.

Over the years, many readers have asked me to clarify and expand upon the teachings presented in my first book. Socrates had, after all, made some outrageous statements and paradoxical references — for example, when he railed against moderation, or answered my questions with a shrug and the enigmatic response "It's the House Rules."

It wasn't until 2006, as the *Peaceful Warrior* movie was about to open, that I realized the time had come to shed new light on the peaceful warrior's way. That decision gave birth to *Wisdom of the Peaceful Warrior*, which contains key dialogue and incidents from *Way of the Peaceful Warrior*, followed by commentaries to deepen and illuminate the original teachings.

I encourage you to read these words as if Socrates himself had written them. Because, in a paradoxical way, perhaps he did.

Dan Millman
Summer 2006

WISDOM OF THE
PEACEFUL WARRIOR

ON THE PREFACE TO

WAY OF THE PEACEFUL WARRIOR

The Road goes ever on and on
Down from the door where it began,
Now far ahead the Road has gone,
And I must follow, if I can,
Pursuing it with eager feet,
Until it joins some larger way
Where many paths and errands meet,
And whither then? I cannot say.

— J. R. R. TOLKIEN

Reality Check 1

An extraordinary series of events took place in my life, beginning in December 1966, during my junior year at the University of California at Berkeley. It all began at 3:20 a.m., when I first stumbled upon Socrates in an all-night gas station.

I've taken great care over the years to clarify that *Way of the Peaceful Warrior* blends fact and fiction, memoir and invention, autobiography and imagination. To avoid confusion, the back cover categorizes the book as "Personal Growth/Fiction."

Pablo Picasso once said, "Art is a lie that helps us see the truth." This raises some larger questions: What is truth? What is reality? We're advised to trust our senses, yet whatever we perceive only reflects our personal or subjective reality filtered through our beliefs, associations, and interpretations.

Even the most intelligent among us can mistake printed words and televised images for reality or truth. For example, an acquaintance told me how she had witnessed one of the two World Trade Center towers collapsing on September 11, 2001, from her Manhattan apartment balcony. She couldn't believe her eyes, so she ran into her apartment and *turned on her television to see if it was real.* And some of us believe that certain advanced yogis can appear in two places at the same time, or that a few great saints have levitated — not because we've witnessed such events, but because we have read or heard about them. Perhaps such phenomena really happen, but do they become "facts" because they appear in print?

Aspects of objective reality, such as gravity, remain true whether or not we believe in them. But in the subjective realm of faith, and when navigating the flowing waters of spirituality, it's wise to cultivate discernment, critical thinking, and common sense. So read *Way of the Peaceful Warrior* and other spiritual literature to enjoy the stories, inspiration, and transcendental reminders, but always temper faith with reason and trust your direct experience.

Disillusion: The Search Begins

Life brought rewards, but no lasting peace or satisfaction.

This statement, which describes the emptiness that began my search for spirit, has also drawn millions of readers into the story. Most of us share a yearning for "something more," even when we cannot fathom or articulate what that "something more" might be. As the nineteenth-century transcendentalist Henry David Thoreau wrote, "Some men go fishing all their lives without realizing that it is not fish they are after."

We seek a liberating glimpse of life's bigger picture, a sense of peace and fulfillment that transcends the stuff of ordinary life. This is the universal promise of religion, spirituality, the inner quest. The compelling urge that once drew American pioneers west now calls them to the mysterious East.

Today, teeming millions in developing nations around the world still struggle daily for survival; that is their primary quest. As Mahatma Gandhi reminded us, "To a starving man, God is bread."

However, those of us fortunate enough to live in more comfortable circumstances, where food and shelter are relatively secure, have the time, attention, and energy to strive for higher aspirations — for fulfillment, meaning, and self-actualization.

Those of us who have traveled far on the extroverted Western path of achievement, success, material wealth, status, and possessions (or who have seen our parents pursue such rewards and comforts) have noticed that such external benefits do not bestow peace or happiness.

Those of us disillusioned with outer success have turned to the more internalized Eastern path — detachment from money, possessions, status, and outward achievement. We simplify our lives, cut away external trappings and symbols, and look for our answers within. We may meditate and explore various introspective paths of esoteric knowledge. Such inward-focused seekers often have their own difficulties dealing with worldly responsibilities, such as paying the rent, maintaining a household, or finding stable work.

Thus, the peaceful warrior's way embraces the virtues of both West and East, outer and inner, flesh and spirit, left brain and right brain, head and heart, reason and faith, science and mysticism, modern technology and indigenous wisdom, the conventional and the transcendental. Life is not an either/or proposition, but rather an integration of apparent dualities. As peaceful warriors, we each keep our head in the clouds but our feet on the ground; we strive for a peaceful heart *and* a warrior spirit.

This approach may not guarantee permanent peace or satisfaction — nothing can, since emotions pass like the weather — but it represents a realistic and balanced way to live.

How Shall We Live?

I never suspected that I would have to learn how to live — that there were specific disciplines and ways of seeing the world I had to master before I could awaken to a simple, happy, uncomplicated life.

The conventional mind, represented in such films as *Pleasantville* and *The Truman Show*, is founded upon agreed-upon illusions. Such illusions are appealing on the surface but mask what Thoreau referred to as "lives of quiet desperation." We used to believe that if we earned good grades in school, worked at nice jobs, got married, and had 1.5 children apiece — if we did what was expected of us — we could look forward to the weekends and holidays and retirement, and life would be full and good.

To some degree, such ordinary pleasures are indeed part of a good life. But not if we sleepwalk through it all — not if we become drones educated only by conventional beliefs and the mainstream media.

The way of the peaceful warrior and other paths of wisdom are founded upon the proposition that there are higher ways to view the world, as well as time-tested practices for balancing and integrating body, mind, and spirit.

But what disciplines and perspectives do we need to master before we can awaken? Are they hidden, esoteric practices for only a monk-like few sitting in caves meditating, generating inner heat, or sending kundalini energy up their spines?

Or are these disciplines right in front of us, here and now, in our daily lives, such as learning to accept our thoughts and emotions instead of struggling to fix them, and behaving responsibly, constructively, and kindly whether or not we feel like it?

Such daily practice is the core of what I teach. We're all peaceful warriors in training — right here, right now.

Reality Check 2

This story is based on my adventure, but it is a novel. The man I called Socrates did, in fact, exist. Yet he had a way of blending into the world, so it's been difficult at times to tell where he left off and other teachers and life experiences began. I have taken liberties with the dialogue and with some time sequences and have sprinkled anecdotes and metaphors into the story to highlight the lessons Socrates would want me to convey.

Socrates was indeed a real person. When we met, he reminded me of the ancient Greek sage, so I called him by that name.

More than a decade passed between our first meeting and the publication of my first book. During that time I traveled widely, met other mentors and masters, and gained further clarity, perspective, and maturity in the school of daily life. So, when I finally sat down to write *Way of the Peaceful Warrior*, the service station sage I called Socrates spoke for many teachers and expressed that cumulative wisdom.

Let's turn now to the opening of the story, after I drove off to college to start a new life — a life that shifted abruptly when I wandered into that old Texaco station and stumbled upon my destiny.

ON THE
GAS STATION AT RAINBOW'S END

One chance is all you need.

—— JESSE OWENS

A Turning Point

"Life begins," I thought, as I waved good-bye to Mom and Dad and pulled away from the curb in my reliable old Valiant, its faded white body stuffed with the belongings I'd packed for my first year at college. I felt strong, independent, ready for anything.

Life unfolds moment to moment in what some view as a constant flow. But in our human experience there seem to be turning points, when doors open where none were previously visible. Driving up to Berkeley to begin my college years felt like one of those times. I was on top of the world and filled with optimism. My gymnastics teammates were waiting for me at the gym — promising new friends and possibilities.

I had no idea at all — no clue — about what else, or who else, was waiting. Registration lines and classes, new routines and workouts, claimed my attention for several years. Then the dark dreams began, eventually sending me into Soc's old gas station.

Reality Check 3

When I reached the curb, I stopped. My neck tingled; I felt that he was watching me. I glanced back. No more than fifteen seconds had passed. But there he was, standing on the roof, his arms crossed, looking up at the starry sky. I gaped at the empty chair still leaning back against the wall, then up again. It was impossible! If he had been changing a wheel on a carriage made from a giant pumpkin drawn by huge mice, the effect couldn't have been any more startling.

As I've said, I based *Way of the Peaceful Warrior* on numerous events from my life, along with elements of imagination.

I never actually saw Socrates jump up on the gas station roof. As I described it in the book, Soc was sitting in a chair — then, a short time later, he was up on the roof. Later in the book, Soc touched my head and I saw him, or thought I saw him, leap up, as if in slow motion, to the rooftop. But that vision could have come from a sort of hypnosis. Did I see what I wanted to see, or what Soc wanted me to see? All of these questions exist within the subtext of the story.

What if, instead of possessing great leaping abilities, Socrates had learned from a shaman how to alter someone else's sense of time, so that instead of a few seconds passing as I was walking away from the station, a few minutes had actually gone by, giving Soc plenty of time to climb up to (and later down from) the roof?

To paraphrase the principle of Occam's razor, attributed to Franciscan friar William of Occam, the simplest theory is often the best explanation. So we might simply agree that I included various magical elements and leaps of faith in service of the larger story. As described in the book, Socrates created some unusual experiences to hold my interest; I chose to do the same for my readers.

What drew me to Socrates was not a rooftop leap but something more basic and profound. There's a famous story about a wanderer who encountered Gautama the Buddha out walking and sensed something special about him. "Are you a warrior?" he asked. Gautama shook his head. "Are you a magician?" When Gautama indicated no, the man persisted: "Well, are you a king or a sage?" Again the Buddha shook his head, so the wanderer pressed on: "Then what is it that makes you different from other men?" he asked.

"I am awake," the Buddha replied.

To the dreamer, finding someone awake within the dream is quite an astonishing thing. That alone drew me like the moth to Soc's light; that alone changed the course of my life.

Fools Together

"So you think I'm a fool?" I said, sounding more belligerent than I'd intended.

"We're all fools together," he replied. "It's just that a few people know it; others don't. You seem to be one of the latter types."

In the tarot — a sacred set of cards depicting in archetypal images the human journey of experience, evolution, and awakening

— the first card in the major arcana is the Fool. This card shows a jester (representing the innocent child) gazing up at the sun, about to step over a cliff (falling into the complications of life).

This is the Fool to which Socrates was referring — the innocent, the naive, those blinded by the light and thinking all sorts of idealistic notions, filled with untested beliefs, awash in self-deception. Few of us escape this fall from grace; it seems to be an inherent part of our human journey.

We all wish that our children might bypass this fall from grace and remain innocent, open, and spontaneous — that they might avoid the obstacle-laden path of life. But it's a necessary journey we all take — this Fool's adventure — gaining wisdom on the way, all in preparation for our ultimate destiny.

Short of enlightenment, we remain sleepwalkers in a subjective reality of our own creation. Yet the term *fool* seems a harsh one to apply helter-skelter, so let's just say that we each have our foolish moments, our intelligent moments, our cruel moments, our kind moments, our crazy moments, our peaceful moments.

Socrates never intended to imply that I was a stupid lout. He was addressing my self-image, and my illusions of "having it all together." He knew I had to lose face, let go, and encounter my shadow side and fears before I could open to something more. The same is true for any of us. As Soc once said, "Before you become spiritual, you have to become a mature human."

Sleeping, Dreaming, and Waking

"How do you know you haven't been asleep your whole life? How do you know you're not asleep right now?" he said, watching me intently.

A good method for learning the art of *lucid dreaming* — waking up within a dream — is to ask yourself, at random moments during the day: "Am I dreaming this?" Most of the time, after asking this question, you'll answer, "No, I'm not dreaming." But there may come a time, after you've formed the habit of asking this question, when you realize that you really *are* dreaming. You instantly become lucid — that is, awake — within the dream.

In this state of lucid dreaming, you can then consciously create the dream rather than being a passive player: You can fly or turn the monster into a daisy if you wish. This process of lucid dreaming is quite ancient. The Tibetan monks practiced it, calling it *working the bardo* — exploring the dreamlike space between lifetimes, after death and before the next rebirth, according to their cosmology.

There's a higher meaning to this metaphor of sleeping, dreaming, and waking up. Awakened teachers suggest that in the same way we sleep and dream at night, then wake up in the morning, in our waking lives we move about confused, stumbling from one experience to the next, lost in our beliefs, associations, and interpretations about reality, much as if we were dreaming.

Until we can perceive reality as it is, without all the extras, meanings, and complications, we slumber through our nights and sleepwalk through our days, dreaming our lives away in a reality of our own creation.

Doorways to Dreaming

"You know, Socrates, I feel as though I've met you before."

"You have," he answered, again opening the doorway in my mind where dreams and reality become one. I paused.

"Uh, Socrates, I've been having this dream — you're in it." I watched him carefully, but his face revealed nothing.

"I've been in many people's dreams; so have you. Tell me about your dream."

In *Way of the Peaceful Warrior* I wrote a lot about dreaming — that dark wellspring of the psyche, which Sigmund Freud referred to as "the royal road to the unconscious." My meetings with Socrates served as a bridge between the world of dreams — the realm of the unconscious — and everyday reality. Shamans and mystics also travel across this bridge between worlds, as do people suffering from schizophrenia — the difference being that shamans and mystics move consciously between these worlds and understand the difference between the two; those with mental illnesses do not.

In both the book and the movie, Dan receives many dream messages from the netherworld. Within that reality, Socrates apparently travels freely, like the shamanic aboriginal people from Malaysia, the Senoi, for whom dreaming is as real as, or more real than, waking life, and who ask their children every morning to relate their dreams, then nearly always respond, "A good dream!"

Most of us have experienced that déjà vu sense that we have seen someone before, or even dreamed of something, that later came to pass. Many of us don't recall or pay much attention to our dreams, and some of us even believe that we don't dream at all. But everyone has a rich dream life, which we can access through a willingness to awaken in the darkness and jot down some notes. Sometimes our dream messages have hidden or symbolic meanings, and sometimes their only message is that we ate too much pizza before bedtime.

In any case, my experiences with Socrates provided me

with greater awareness of the realm of dreams and the unconscious. He lived fully in both worlds, while I had not yet awakened in either one.

A Living Example

Some of the people were in a party mood, laughing loudly and blaring their radios while we waited on them. Socrates laughed right along with them. One or two customers were sullen, putting forth a special effort to be unpleasant, but Socrates treated one and all with the same courtesy — as if each person were his personal guest.

Author James Baldwin once wrote, "Children have never been very good at listening to what their parents tell them, but they never fail to imitate them." The same is true of adults. As time passed I observed how Socrates ate, moved, and breathed. His simple relations with others taught me more than his words ever could. He treated every customer, young or old, with the courtesy and respect he might have shown an honored guest.

Of course, there were exceptions, which I relate in the book, when Soc played the eccentric, but even then his actions were always conscious and deliberate — a part of his paradoxical method of instruction, for my sake or for the sake of others.

How different might our own lives look and feel if we could remember that within all the people we meet — no matter how irritating their personalities at any given moment — stirs a soul like our own, yearning for the light?

What Socrates taught me without words reminds me of something the great humanitarian and physician Albert Schweitzer once said: "Example is not the main thing in influencing others. It is the only thing."

Practical Wisdom: Student and Teacher

"I still want to know what we can do for each other."

"Just this: I wouldn't mind having one last student, and you obviously need a teacher."

"I have enough teachers," I said too quickly.

He paused and drew a deep breath. *"Whether you have a proper teacher or not depends upon what you want to learn."*

Socrates was not anti-intellectual. He had a measure of respect for those with academic credentials, but he avoided putting credentials on a pedestal. He understood the strengths and limitations represented by a degree. He once cited one of the many quips he had heard on this and nearly every other subject: "An expert is someone who knows more and more about less and less until he knows everything about nothing."

Advanced degrees often require years of study; this means someone has passed through a cerebral gauntlet and undergone rigorous initiation into the world of the intellect. Such study is a real achievement, worthy of respect, but Socrates was quick to point out the difference between conceptual knowledge and practical wisdom.

He once told me the story of a young Indian scholar who had paid a ferryman to take him across a deep, surging river. They struck up a conversation as the young scholar, glancing with concern at the surging water, told the humble ferryman about his studies and academic accomplishments. Then the ferryman asked, "During your schooling, did you ever learn to swim?"

"No," answered the youth.

"That's too bad," said the ferryman, "because this boat is sinking."

If we want to get in shape for a marathon, that entails one

kind of training; if we have a more modest goal, such as being able to walk up a set of stairs without getting winded, that involves a less rigorous form of training. Similarly, the sort of teacher we need depends on what we want to learn. The important thing is to find mentors who have traveled the paths and ascended the mountains we wish to climb. When you find teachers who seem to meet your needs, listen well but observe even more acutely — because their example will always be more important than their words.

Daily Life as a Divine School

"The world out there," he said, waving his arm across the horizon, "is a school, Dan. Life is the only real teacher. It offers many experiences, and if experience alone brought wisdom and fulfillment, then elderly people would all be happy, enlightened masters. But the lessons of experience are hidden. I can help you learn from experience to see the world clearly."

Like Socrates, I view this planet as a divine school, and daily life as our classroom. The challenges we meet along the way — in personal and business relationships, in health, finances, and career — and the consequences of our actions are guaranteed to teach us all we need in order to evolve. Daily life provides the spiritual weight lifting that strengthens our spirits as we ascend the mountain path.

In other words, *the way itself creates the warrior.* As our course work continues, lessons repeat themselves until we learn them. And if we don't learn the easy lessons, they get harder. As the saying goes, "Experience is the best teacher, but her fees can be high."

Every soul must travel through both light and darkness.

Teachers and guides can only light the way and provide maps of the territory, reminding us of what we all know at deeper levels but tend to forget. We forget, then remember, then forget again; we stumble and fall and rise again, ever onward, two steps forward, one step back. This, too, is the way.

Experience and Wisdom

"You haven't yet turned knowledge into wisdom."

Preoccupied with debating Socrates, stuck in my conceptual mind, I was idly flipping a squeegee that Soc had given me to clean a car windshield with when I asked him what he meant by the difference between knowledge and wisdom. He answered, "You know how to clean the windshield; wisdom is doing it."

We can know about any number of things, and gather facts and data and sophisticated information from other people, and from books, newspapers, and the Internet. But wisdom flows from life experience. Wisdom takes on the taste of sweat as we strive to overcome lower tendencies and live in accordance with universal laws — or "the House Rules," as Soc called them.

Body Wisdom

"What are you going to do, fill me full of your facts?" I bristled.

"It's not a matter of facts; it's a matter of body wisdom."

"What's 'body wisdom'?"

"Everything you'll ever need to know is within you; the secrets of the universe are imprinted on the cells of your body. But you haven't learned how to read the wisdom of the body. So you can only read books and listen to experts and hope they are right."

Taisen Deshimaru, a Japanese sword master, once said, "Learn to think with your whole body." He was recommending a different way of being, doing, and living in the world — making decisions instantly, instinctually, and intuitively rather than relying solely on the brain to weigh variables and figure things out.

Socrates, like Deshimaru, understood the innate (and instantaneous) wisdom of the body. He had trained, and had come to trust, his body's knowledge about what to eat, how to exercise, and how to respond to each moment freshly, without expectation or judgment. As one of Soc's mentors said (in *The Journeys of Socrates*), "Expect nothing, but be prepared for anything."

Understanding and Realization

"Understanding is the one-dimensional comprehension of the intellect. It leads to knowledge. Realization is three-dimensional — a simultaneous comprehension of head, heart, and instinct. It comes only from direct experience."

As the proverb goes, "I hear and I forget; I see and I remember; I do and I understand." In this case, the word *understand* refers to "realizing," because doing leads to realization. To study the principles of mountain climbing is to gain conceptual knowledge; to climb a mountain is to experience direct realization.

We can all comprehend the idea behind the statements "Everything is a dream" and "We don't actually know what anything is." Hearing such concepts, we may notice only their surface meanings and say, "I know that already." Or "I agree" or "I disagree." We may shrug off such proverbs as clichés simply because we have heard similar phrases many times.

But when such ideas truly penetrate our psyches, they change from mere bromides to universal truths — and we *realize* that everything is a dream, or truly grasp that we really *do not know what anything is*. Such sudden and life-changing moments can generate an ecstatic sense of liberation from mortality, from change, from suffering. We may even burst out laughing. It's the same sense of excitement that caused the Greek mathematician Archimedes, in a fit of jubilation as he experienced a scientific insight, to leap straight out of the bath and run naked down the streets shouting "*Eureka*! I've found it!"

Nothing changes, yet everything changes — in a single moment of realization.

Ignorance and Mystery and Bliss

"Where are you?" he repeated softly.

"I'm here."

"Where is here?"

"In this office, in this gas station!" I was getting impatient with this game.

"Where is this gas station?"

"In Berkeley?"

"Where is Berkeley?"

"In California."

"Where is California?"

"In the United States."

"Where is the United States?"

"On a landmass, one of the continents in the Western Hemisphere. Socrates, I..."

"Where are the continents?" ...

I sighed. *"On the earth...in the solar system...in the Milky Way...."*

"And where . . . is the universe?" . . .

"I don't know — how can I answer that?"

"That is the point. You cannot answer it, and you never will. There is no knowing about it. You are ignorant of where the universe is, and thus, where you are. In fact, you have no knowledge of where anything is or what anything is or how it came to be. Life is a mystery.

"My ignorance, Dan, is based on this understanding. Your understanding is based on ignorance. This is why I am a humorous fool, and you are a serious jackass."

The ancient Greek philosopher Socrates, my mentor's namesake, claimed to be "the most ignorant of men." And since those days with my own Socrates, I can make the same claim: I possess no certain or ultimate knowledge — not a smidgen, not a drop. All my "facts" are but a house of cards, balanced atop a realm of wonder.

We can amass a vast storehouse of facts and theories and verifiable conclusions, but underlying all that knowledge we remain children gazing into infinity. Newspaperman and perennial cynic H. L. Mencken once wrote, "We are here and it is now. Beyond that, all human knowledge is moonshine." Mencken could hardly be mistaken for a spiritual teacher, yet he also pointed to the mystery at the core of life.

Knowing and Doing

"Dan, I have places to show you and tales to tell. I have secrets to unfold. But before we begin this journey together, you must appreciate that a secret's value is not in what you know, but in what you do."

Soc took an old dictionary from his drawer and held it in the air. "Use whatever knowledge you have but see its limitations. Knowledge alone does not suffice; it has no heart. No amount of knowledge will nourish or sustain your spirit; it can never bring you ultimate happiness or peace. Life requires more than knowledge; it requires intense feeling and constant energy. Life demands right action if knowledge is to come alive."

We're all familiar with the old saying "It isn't what you know, but what you do, that counts." And "Life is about the journey, not the destination." And "You can lead a horse to water..." But as I mentioned earlier, *knowing* something is not the same as *living* it.

We all know about the benefits of a balanced diet, regular exercise, and sufficient rest. These are not secrets locked away in esoteric volumes or monastery vaults. We read all sorts of good advice in daily newspapers and popular magazines. But the point of all this advice remains hidden from us until we take action. Of course, there are also times when stillness (the action of nonaction) is an appropriate response. In any case, the peaceful warrior doesn't act without thinking, or think without acting.

What additional secret might Socrates reveal about how to turn knowledge into action? I think he would put down his socket wrench, wipe his hands, and say, "Dream big, but start small. Then connect the dots."

The Way of Action

He sat up on the floor and turned to face me, making a final point. "Your feelings and reactions, Dan, are automatic and predictable; mine are not. I create my life spontaneously; yours is determined by your thoughts, your emotions, your past."

Time and again Socrates said it: "This is a way of action." By that, I thought he meant being active, strong, dynamic, and forthright — not holding back, not wobbling, but acting decisively. Most of my readers have thought the same.

But Socrates was actually referring to an approach to reality so radical that I wouldn't fully grasp it until nearly three decades had passed: He was aware that our emotions, thoughts, beliefs, and memories all create tendencies within us to behave in certain ways. For example, if we're feeling sad or angry or afraid, or just plain bad about ourselves, we *tend* to behave differently than we'd behave if we were feeling happy and confident. Most of us live soap-opera lives — slaves to our tendencies, hoping that we'll have the right emotions and thoughts to "allow" us to behave differently, and fearing that the wrong emotions or thoughts might block us from our goals.

For years I used my emotions and my past as reasons for behaving as I did. Socrates pulled the rug out from under my excuses by insisting that I reclaim the power to behave with courage and compassion no matter what I was feeling or thinking.

That's why Socrates focused on the body, the doing, the behavior. Thoughts and emotions, both positive and negative, flowed through him without apparent resistance or attachment, no longer driving his actions. He was free to behave according to a higher will.

In demonstrating his freedom from his inner, subjective world and his underlying tendencies, Socrates showed me a new way of living — the way of action, the way of the peaceful warrior.

A Long-Awaited Meeting

"How can you assume all this about me, about my past?"
"Because, I've been watching you for years."

Soc's response that he had been watching me was, to paraphrase Winston Churchill, a riddle wrapped in a mystery inside an enigma. He said it almost casually, as if it were a perfectly reasonable thing to say. He didn't explain it to me, nor could I shed any light on it for my readers — at least not until twenty-five years later, when I wrote *The Journeys of Socrates*, which relates the life and odyssey of my old mentor.

As was customary for Socrates, I offer a hint here rather than a full elucidation: Suffice it to say that Soc had known of my existence and kept track of my movements from my birth until the time I moved to Berkeley to begin my college studies. He had bought that old gas station not long after I arrived. While he never met my mother, he did know my grandmother — not as well as he would have wished, but well enough.

In a sense, our first meeting at the gas station was both chance and fate. I walked in of my own accord, but he had been waiting patiently for me for many years.

Trusting the Inner Knower

I stood, ready to leave. "Socrates, you've told me to listen to my own body intuition and not depend upon what I read or what people tell me. Why, then, should I sit quietly and listen to what you tell me?"

"A very good question," he answered. "There is an equally good answer. First of all, I speak to you from my own experience; I am not relating abstract theories I read in a book or heard secondhand from an expert. I am one who truly knows his own body and mind, and therefore knows others' as well. Besides," he smiled, "how do you know that I'm not your own intuition, speaking to you now?"

This dialogue sequence raises an important question about trust. Socrates wasn't an Eastern guru who demanded absolute surrender when I walked in the door. He was my mentor — a wise elder and source of challenge and counsel.

Soc recognized that trust is best earned over time, not given on blind faith or as a show of devotion. He once told me, "I'm not here for you to trust me; I'm here to help you trust yourself." I share this same purpose — not to present my way, but to help you find your own.

True teachers welcome disagreement and questions. After all, if we already agree on everything, only one of us is necessary.

Soc's statement implying that he was somehow my own intuition speaking to me pointed to his uncanny ability to look beneath the surface. Even as I paid attention to my conscious mind — what I *thought* I wanted — Soc was tuning in and giving expression to my heart's deepest longings and needs.

I would later learn that he had developed this capacity by training with a woman named Chia many years before — the same woman I would eventually meet in a Hawaiian rain forest, as I describe in *Sacred Journey of the Peaceful Warrior*, the second book in the series.

Soc's Martial Arts Lineage

"The ninja could swim wearing heavy armor; they could climb sheer walls like lizards, using only fingers and toes in tiny cracks. They designed imaginative scaling ropes, dark and nearly invisible, and used clever means of hiding, tricks of distraction, illusion, and escape. The ninja," he finally added, "were great jumpers."

Way of the Peaceful Warrior readers will recall the story Socrates told me when I demanded an explanation for how he had gotten on the roof — about how young ninjas of Japan practice jumping over cornstalks each day, and that he practiced with gas stations.

Because Soc referred to the ninja, many readers have assumed that he had studied the martial skills of *ninjutsu*. Some even assumed that Socrates was Asian. That was not the case. As detailed in *The Journeys of Socrates*, he came from Russia and had mastered a traditional martial art that is today called *systema*.

Some Westerners assume that spiritual wisdom comes only from Japan, China, or India. These and other cultures, such as those of the Islamic Sufis, African *sangomas*, and Hawaiian kahunas, have great esoteric traditions. But Soc's wisdom came from the rivers and trees, from the clouds and changing seasons; he conveyed the wisdom of the earth, which is found everywhere and belongs to all of us.

And as I've already noted, Soc's sudden appearance on the roof was not a ninja feat so much as an attention-getting device to keep me around long enough to learn something — as well as a literary device to pique my readers' interest.

Becoming Responsible

"When you become fully responsible for your life, you can become fully human; once you become human, you may discover what it means to be a warrior."

Socrates spoke at great length about taking responsibility, not for our thoughts or feelings, but for our actions. He knew very well that any direct control we have begins and ends with our behavior.

Our place of birth, parents, and external events in the world are beyond our control; so are the feelings and thoughts that pass through our field of awareness. On occasion we may be able to snap out of bad moods or shift our attention from unpleasant thoughts or feelings until they pass, but no one I know can consistently change every emotion or filter out all negative thoughts.

Unless we have a related disability, we have control over, and responsibility for, how we move our own body parts and what we say. Once we take responsibility for what we do and say (no matter what thoughts or feelings arise), we reach a new stage of personal evolution.

Some of us believe that difficult childhoods, or lack of positive role models, or failure to bond with our mothers may generate negative behaviors in adolescents or adults. Such factors undoubtedly create psychological hurdles, yet many people who have faced such circumstances nonetheless respond to life's challenges in productive, positive ways.

So it comes to this: No matter what our past experiences, except in the case of severe delusion and mental illness, we retain the power to choose the best course of action we can, within the context of our environment and circumstances. But reclaiming the power to choose requires resolve and fortitude. That's why becoming fully human — overcoming our primitive tendencies — is the biggest challenge we face. "After you become fully human," Soc once said, "the rest is an elevator ride." Meanwhile, every day offers the opportunity to develop a peaceful heart and a warrior spirit.

ON BOOK ONE
THE WINDS OF CHANGE

We are changing — we have got to change —
we can no more help it
than leaves can help going yellow
and coming loose in autumn.

— D. H. LAWRENCE

ON CHAPTER ONE

GUSTS OF MAGIC

Do not be a magician;
be magic.

— LEONARD COHEN

The Shaman's Reality

"Yes, the winds. They're changing. It means a turning point for you
— now. You may not have realized it; neither did I, in fact — but
tonight is a critical moment in time for you. You left, but you re-
turned. And now the winds are changing." He looked at me for a
moment, then strode back inside.

Among the chameleon roles played by Socrates (from stern
taskmaster to humorous eccentric), he excelled in playing the
shaman — one who travels in the shadow lands, a wayfarer in
the depths of the subconscious mind. The shaman divines

meanings and messages from the whispers of the natural world and can translate them for others. In that capacity, Soc made much of omens and signs from nature, and the shifting winds spoke to him of coming changes in my life.

Some say that all of this is mere superstition — a play of the mind, a throwback to primitive cultures. But I believe that ancient peoples may hold valuable perspectives for modern lives cut off from primal rhythms that speak to the cells of our bodies.

All young children are shamans, but they wander in dreamscapes they do not understand. In contrast, trained intuitives use oracular tools such as astrological signs, tarot cards, Nordic runes, or other devices as conscious ways to focus their sight, just as shamans use the natural world as their oracle. Nature whispers secrets to the shaman when others hear only the wind.

Accepting Change

"Don't be afraid," he repeated. "Comfort yourself with a saying of Confucius," he smiled. " 'Only the supremely wise and the ignorant do not alter.'" Saying that, he reached out and placed his hands gently but firmly on my temples.

When Socrates quoted that old Confucian proverb, he meant that the ignorant are like stones and the wise are like water. Stones do not change; they only break or wear down over time. Yet water remains the same as it adapts perfectly to the shape of its container; even when moving from ice to liquid to gas, its essential nature remains.

The wise among us retain their balance while surfing the waves of change; they navigate effortlessly down even the most powerful rivers. They represent the still center of the raging hurricane.

Those of us who are unhappy with our lives may wish for a change in our environment or in the people around us. But when life is good (or sometimes even not so good), we often resist change due to fear of the unknown. We also resist the natural changes brought by passing years. (Never mind aging gracefully; we don't want to age at all!) But change is one of the House Rules that govern all of life.

Despite all our hopes and efforts and strategies, change is indeed the only constant. Consider this quotation by Lewis Carroll from *Alice's Adventures in Wonderland*:

> "Who are you?" asked the Caterpillar.
>
> "I-I hardly know, Sir, just at present," Alice replied, rather shyly. "I knew who I was when I got up this morning, but I think I must have changed several times since then."

Eventually we all learn the inevitability of change and the wisdom of flexibility and acceptance, since nothing stays the same. Until then, we resist, and such resistance creates stress, suffering, and pain.

But pain generates learning. We've all experienced physical, emotional, and mental pain — and many times adversity has left us a little stronger, wiser, and more compassionate. As the existential writer Albert Camus wrote, "In the midst of winter I discovered within me an invincible summer." Our souls make the greatest strides in the face of difficulty: a bankruptcy, a divorce, an illness, an injury, a death in the family. Such challenges forge our characters and temper our spirits — for our highest good and learning.

Opening the Doors of Perception

"Let's just say I manipulated your energies and opened a few new circuits. The fireworks were just your brain's delight in the energy bath. The result is that you are relieved of your lifelong illusion of knowledge. From now on, ordinary knowledge is no longer going to satisfy you, I'm afraid."...

The next day was full of classes and full of professors babbling words that had no meaning or relevance for me. In History 101, Watson lectured on how Churchill's political instincts had affected the war. I stopped taking notes. I was too busy taking in the colors and textures of the room, feeling the energies of the people around me. The sounds of my professors' voices were far more interesting than the concepts they conveyed.

This incident from the book and a similar scene in the *Peaceful Warrior* movie depict Socrates transmitting some sort of energy to heighten my perceptions and open circuits to stimulate a psychedelic effect. Did Socrates have an implied right to do what he did? Should he have asked permission first? How could he presume to know what was best for my evolution? Did he cross boundaries and interfere with my process, or enhance it?

By this time in the narrative, Socrates and I had developed a student-mentor relationship. Just as psychotherapists might use hypnosis or other methods from their toolbox of techniques, Soc did the same. Only his toolbox was something special, based on his training, some of which I describe in *The Journeys of Socrates*.

I related this incident in *Way of the Peaceful Warrior* to draw a distinction between the different kinds of knowledge — academic concepts versus practical wisdom based upon direct experience. Science and reason reflect the left brain; mysticism is the domain of the right brain. The peaceful warrior doesn't choose between the two, but integrates both.

Socrates helped to clear my head of abstract academic concepts, and to develop a more direct relationship with reality. Previous to this time, I perceived the world through a veil of thoughts and recycled impressions. Socrates helped me to hit the refresh button and empty the cache in my brain. My world came alive once again; a distorted, black-and-white existence came into focus and turned to color.

Transcending Conventional Agreements

"Hey," she said. "Wasn't Watson's lecture great? I just love hearing about Churchill's life. Isn't it interesting?"

"Uh, yeah — great lecture."

In this snippet of dialogue between Susie and me, Susie represents the familiar, agreed-upon conventional reality most of us find so comfortable — the consolations and pleasures of food and sex and entertainment — diversions to keep the mind busy as we live typical lives filled with news, weather reports, and sports.

Seduced by the siren call of being a regular guy, of fitting in, I felt the familiar urge to return to agreed upon social ideas — to fall back to sleep and abandon my foolish search for something more.

But after my experiences with Socrates, I found I couldn't go back, as much as I might have wanted to. And even as I numbly agreed with Susie that the lecture was "great," I realized I didn't believe it — not anymore. Of course, there's nothing wrong with going to college or attending informative lectures about history, philosophy, or any other area of human knowledge. It's just that after what I had experienced, mere information felt flat and dry and two-dimensional. I knew what real "higher education" meant, because I had found it in the form of an unlikely old gas station mechanic who happened to be awake. Thus, as a result of Soc's intervention, I felt a growing gap between the conventional world and the transcendent.

The Darkness before the Dawn

"Aren't you supposed to make things better for me? I thought that's what a teacher did."

As my question to Socrates implied, I had expected a payoff for my efforts in going through his wringer. Things were supposed to feel better, but it seemed as if I was only getting worse. This phenomenon of things seeming to get worse before they get better is common, even necessary, and it doesn't occur just in the arena of spiritual practice. We experience this disillusioning perception in any process that involves growth or progress in a high-skill activity — whether sports or music or martial arts training.

When I first began studying aikido, my sensei, or instructor, would keep reminding me to relax. I found this frustrating, because I thought I was relaxing — but in light of my instructor's reminders, it seemed I was getting more tense than ever. My standards had gone up, as had my awareness of the problem: tension. But with my depressing and growing awareness of the tension came the possibility of truly relaxing. Awareness of the problem is the beginning of the solution.

Like an airplane rising up through the clouds, we often experience turbulence as our awareness rises to a new level. We realize what is possible, we raise our sights and standards, and we see ourselves more clearly. Often it appears darkest before the dawn — even within the human psyche.

Owning the Power of Choice

"And another thing. I've always believed that we have to find our own paths in life. No one can tell another how to live."

Socrates slapped his forehead with his palm, then looked upward in resignation. "I am part of your path, baboon. And I didn't exactly rob you from the cradle and lock you up here, you know. You can take off whenever you like."

A childlike part of me wanted a wise teacher, but the adolescent in me rebelled. Pulled between "trusting my teacher" and "trusting myself," I repeated my concern about Soc "telling me how to live," since only *I* knew what was best for me.

Socrates had no interest in debating this, so he reminded me that I was not a captive audience: I could leave at any time. This realization helped me stop whining and resisting and begin to take responsibility for my choices. I was not Soc's pawn or victim; I was choosing the experience.

If we compare our lives to a movie, there are times — maybe even lifetimes — when we view ourselves as bit players or stand-ins, waiting for a person or circumstance to dictate what we should do next. We don't act; we only react. I needed the reminder that I could become the director, screenwriter, and star of my movie — my life. We can transform our lives by playing a bigger role.

As peaceful warriors, as mature human beings, we trust life unfolding and see spirit working in and through the people and circumstances in our lives, in the ups and downs, in friends and adversaries. We find wisdom all around us, but we weigh all that we learn, even from trusted teachers, against the counsel of our own hearts.

The Invisible Path of Awareness

"Much of a warrior's path is subtle, invisible to the uninitiated. For now, I have been showing you what a warrior is not by showing you your own mind. You can come to understand that soon enough."

The path of personal evolution isn't showy; no glowing signs identify an evolved being. Such a person may behave in quiet, ordinary ways, or speak with enthusiasm and passion, playing whatever role is called for in the moment. The peaceful warrior is invisible to all but those who can recognize a certain twinkle in the eye, a sense of energy, clarity, and balance. This sense of discernment develops over time as a natural result of inner work. As I came to understand the nature of my own mind and heart, I came to see the light in the minds and hearts of (so-called) others.

Trust in God but Tie Your Camel

Socrates reached into a drawer, took out some long pieces of cotton cloth, and began to tie me to the chair.

Should we allow ourselves to be tied to a chair by a teacher or anyone else? Maybe yes, maybe no — it all depends upon the level of trust established. (If the tying up is done by a stranger on a first date, I wouldn't advise it.) By this point in my student-mentor relationship with Socrates, I was willing to take that risk. I now view Soc's action as a bit of showmanship on his part — he knew how to make an impression, as I've already noted.

As Soc sent me into unknown territory, it felt as if I was about to parachute from an airplane for the first time — I knew it would probably be okay, but it required a leap into the void, an act of faith.

Flights of Imagination

"Are we going flying, Soc?" I asked nervously.

"In a manner of speaking, yes," he said, kneeling in front of me, taking my head in his hands and placing his thumbs against the upper ridges of my eye sockets. My teeth chattered....

We were walking down a corridor swathed in a blue fog. My feet moved but I couldn't feel ground. Gigantic trees surrounded us; they became buildings; the buildings became boulders, and we ascended a steep canyon that became the edge of a sheer cliff.

The fog had cleared; the air was freezing. Green clouds stretched below us for miles, meeting an orange sky on the horizon....

Without warning the clouds disappeared and we were hanging from the rafters of an indoor stadium, swinging precariously like two drunken spiders high above the floor....

"I tied you down so you wouldn't fall off the chair while you were thrashing around playing Peter Pan."

"Did I really fly? I felt like it." I sat down again, heavily.

"Let's say for now that it was a flight of the imagination."

Many people have asked me about the inner journeys generated by Socrates as he laid his hands on my temples. These visionary experiences were in one sense fictional, but in another sense authentic.

As I've mentioned earlier, Socrates did not grab me by the head and generate such experiences. But I did experience such journeys within that mysterious realm we casually call "imagination."

Some people dismiss certain experiences with the phrase "Oh, that's just your imagination," yet Albert Einstein is often quoted as saying, "Imagination is more powerful than knowledge." Why would a brilliant scientist posit such an idea? Perhaps he recognized that all great discoveries come from the human imagination, only later to be tested by the methods of science. Imagination, the source of creativity, is also the bridge to clairvoyant sight. What begin as "flights of fancy" can later tap into subtle cues, signs, and messages from the subconscious, helping us access our deepest intuition.

The visions I described in *Way of the Peaceful Warrior* flowed from my imagination and took on their own reality in my mind, and in yours as you read the words. They became part of our shared experience.

Athletes, musicians, and other performance artists can rehearse and train by imagining themselves accomplishing desired skills. We can cultivate our children's imaginations by reading to them, telling them stories, and encouraging them to tell us stories as well. Those of us with vivid imaginations can pack many lifetimes into one.

When imagination runs wild, in the form of mental illness or hallucinations, we suffer its effects. But if we fully utilize creative imagination — if we harness its visionary powers in the style of mystics and shamans of every culture — we can roam anywhere in the universe, enriching our lives and deepening our experience, freeing ourselves from the limitations of our bodies and our physical senses, and even from time and space. Thus, we use imagination without being seduced by it.

Of course, we also need to ground our imagination in experience, in reality: Making a journey to the jungles of the Amazon is real; imagining that journey is not. Yet dreaming it is far better than never making any journey at all. Flights of fancy reflect one of our greatest human gifts. Then we must return to earth. As Henry David Thoreau wrote, "If you have built castles in the air, your work need not be lost. Now put the foundations under them."

A Doorway Opens

He whispered at me harshly. "This journey is real — more real than the waking dreams of your usual life. Pay attention!"

By this time the scene below had indeed caught my attention. The audience, from this height, coalesced into a multicolored array of dots, a shimmering, rippling, pointillist painting.

Soc's enigmatic words reminded me that there was more than one kind of reality and called me to move beyond my everyday consciousness. But this excerpt also points to a mysterious phenomenon I've never revealed before.

I've often been asked what inspired me to write *Way of the Peaceful Warrior* — as if I had sat down one day and penned the entire book. In reality, the pace and progress of my writing varied considerably over a ten-year period, culminating in an intense effort as I wrote the final draft reframed around my life story. But it all began with a single holographic image that appeared, quite at random, in a moment of reverie. That image was the vision of a stadium seen from a great height, so that the people gathered below appeared as a multicolored array of shimmering dots, as in a pointillist painting.

That odd vision, which appeared as I sat in my office in Philips Gymnasium at Oberlin College, provided a sort of entry point to all that was to follow. The contents of *Way of the Peaceful Warrior* took shape over time, as I began to scribble down notes around that vision and the old man I'd met years before. It was an image so vivid that it stayed imprinted in my memory for many years. The creative process can be as mysterious as that.

Reading Minds

"The acoustics in here," I thought, "must be fantastic." But then I saw that her lips weren't moving....

Somehow, I was reading their minds!

I once asked Socrates if I could learn to read people's minds. He turned to me, raised a bushy white eyebrow, and said, "First you'd better learn to read your own." In other words, until I could clearly see the nature of my own thoughts — see through the filter of my beliefs, associations, and interpretations — I wouldn't be able to perceive anyone or anything else with much clarity.

The higher purpose of this brief dialogue between us was not an invitation to psychic powers or parlor tricks, but a call to explore the nature of mind. By knowing my own mind, I might better empathize with and sense the thoughts and feelings of others.

This power of empathy enables us to connect with others on deeper levels, to become better writers, friends, and human beings — and mature peaceful warriors.

Dynamic Meditation

Furthermore, the best performers had the quietest minds during their moment of truth....

For the first time, I realized why I loved gymnastics so. It gave me a blessed respite from my noisy mind. When I was swinging and somersaulting, nothing else mattered. When my body was active, my mind rested in the moments of silence.

This insight about mind and movement is one of the most important we can realize — it is the foundation of all forms of moving meditation, from the Zen practice of *kinhin*, or walking meditation, to judo or aikido or any active way or path. Many of the Japanese words associated with martial arts end with -do, which means "way" or "path." In fact, the term dojo means "school of the way," where skills are practiced not as an end in themselves but as a means to personal insight and evolution (not merely winning a contest).

Daily life is not lived in a cross-legged posture. Eventually we open our eyes and get on with the day. Thus, sitting meditation is a good beginning, enhanced by moving meditation, which serves as a bridge into everyday life.

In the moment of truth — as we perform our skills in front of an audience, or take a test, or practice any movement skill — our attention rests in the body, on the movement, so our movement becomes our mantra, our focus of attention. That's why I teach juggling at some of my weekend workshops. It's an effective form of meditation, a respite from our busy minds, an instant mental vacation.

Thoughts do not stop arising during such moments of dynamic meditation, but we no longer pay homage to them; they lose their power to distract our attention, drive our moods, or weaken our resolve. During dynamic meditation, we liberate our bodies, for the moment, from the mind. Ultimately, everything we do becomes a dynamic meditation, and we're free from the monkey chatter of random thoughts.

Experience and Imagination

Socrates helped me into the office. As I lay trembling on the couch, I realized that I was no longer the naive and self-important youth who had sat quaking in the gray chair a few minutes or hours or days ago. I felt very old. I had seen the suffering of the world, the condition of the human mind.

This description of a life-changing inner journey was another creation of my imagination, but it came from my life experience. I was not literally transported to another reality by Socrates. As noted earlier, I used this literary device to transmit the teaching in a more visceral way, so understanding could become a sort of realization.

I created incidents, dreams, and visions to bring the messages home about how one naive, self-absorbed young man learned another way of living. And I invited my readers on the adventure, so that my teacher could become theirs.

The Dream of a Lifetime

I awoke to the sound of the windup clock ticking loudly on the blue chest of drawers....

My small feet kicked off the remaining covers, and I leaped out of bed, just as Mom yelled, "Danneeeey — time to get up, sweetheart." It was February 22, 1952 — my sixth birthday....

The years passed, and before long, I was one of the top high school gymnasts in Los Angeles. In the gym, life was exciting; outside the gym, it was a general disappointment....

One day coach Harold Frey called me from Berkeley, California, and offered me a scholarship to the university.... Soon, I was sure, life was really going to begin.

The college years raced by, filled with gymnastics victories but very few other high points. In my senior year, just before the Olympic gymnastics trials, I married Susie. We stayed in Berkeley so I could train with the team; I was so busy I didn't have much time or energy for my new wife....

My newborn son arrived.... I found a job selling life insurance .... Within a year Susie and I were separated; eventually she filed for divorce....

Forty years had passed.... Where had my life gone?...I had overcome my drinking problem; and I'd had money, houses, and women. But I had no one now. I was lonely....

Suddenly I felt a terrible, nagging fear, the worst in my life. Was it possible that I had missed something very important — something that would have made a real difference?

This vision of my childhood, and the empty future I might have lived, provided a sharp impetus for me to persist in this frustrating, confusing path made difficult only through my resistance. That alternate destiny in my dream-vision represented usual, self-focused life — looking for love, happiness, and satisfaction through self-gratification, physical pleasures, disposable entertainment and distractions, and anesthesia poured from a bottle.

To swim across a pond, we have to leave one shore to reach another. Socrates showed me that other shore. Until I reached a point of disillusionment with my future, I would not willingly release the consolations of conventional life and venture into the unknown. That disturbing dream of an empty life served as a wake-up call.

Changing the Past, Changing the Future

"Just as there are different interpretations of the past and many ways to change the present, there are any number of possible futures. What you dreamed was a highly probable future — the one you were headed for had you not met me."

"You mean that if I had decided to pass by the gas station that night, that dream would have been my future?"

"Very possibly. And it still may be. But you can make choices and change your present circumstances. You can alter your future."

When I told Socrates about my dark dream-vision (suspecting that he might already be aware of it), I asked him if that vision foretold my destiny. He reminded me that the only way we can "change our past" is to change our behavior in the present, because the present will soon become our past. We also shape our future by the actions we take right now.

Now is the warrior's moment, and this is a warrior's realization: No matter what we're thinking or feeling — whether we're sad or motivated, shy or assertive, confident or full of doubt — the quality of our lives will always depend, in large part, on what we do today. Today is the doorway to the future; today we build the foundation for what follows.

No Turning Back

"Soc," I said, "I don't know what to make of it. My life these past months has been like an improbable novel, you know what I mean? Sometimes I wish I could go back to a normal life."

My words and wishes in this passage reflect what so many have felt before (or after) making a leap of awareness that seems to distance us from friends or loved ones still living the usual life of sleeping and dreaming and doing what is expected.

Popular culture and film sometimes depict this pull between faux reality and the real thing: *The Matrix* series offers a metaphor depicting the worlds of dreaming and waking up, dramatizing this difference between living in denial and recognizing reality as it is.

Given what I've written, it's easy to conclude that I am disparaging the ordinary conventions of life. This is not the case. Today's politics reflect humanity's current state of awareness and evolution — the best we can do for now. Socrates never told me to reject the conventional activities of life but rather encouraged me to move beyond the *conventional mind* — to realize that there's far more to life than the usual distractions and temporary diversions.

Currently, my personal appearance, clothing, and behaviors appear to be quite conventional. Joy and I live in a suburban home in Northern California with a white picket fence and two cars (although quite old ones at present). We don't live in an ashram or a commune or seclude ourselves in the mountains.

But our values, priorities, and sensibilities are likely different from those of many of our neighbors. It's nothing special — nothing that stands out or sets us apart from the stream of humanity. Just a certain awareness, a lightness, an orientation toward service, and an expanded perspective born of inner work and life experience. And perhaps we display a little less fear, less worry, less resistance. We live in the same world, yet we perceive reality in a slightly different way, even as we pay the bills, mow the lawn, do the laundry. We live as Socrates did — conventional lives, with unconventional perspectives.

THE WEB OF ILLUSION

Losing an illusion makes you wiser
than finding the truth.

— LUDWIG BORNE

Breaking Free

"You don't see your prison because its bars are invisible. Part of my task is to point out your predicament, and I hope it is the most disillusioning experience of your life. . . .

"Disillusion is the greatest gift I can give you . . . a 'freeing from illusion.' . . .

"You are suffering; you do not fundamentally enjoy your life. Your entertainments, your playful affairs, and even your gymnastics are temporary ways to distract you from your underlying sense of fear. . . .

*"You use them to distract you from your chaotic inner life —
the parade of regrets, anxieties, and fantasies you call your mind."*

Imagine looking into a dark well; perhaps some vines or blos-
soms grow along the top, and the depths appear quiet and still.
But when a source of light shines down into the darkness, we
see the creepy-crawlies we were unaware of moments before.
The same phenomenon happens when light shines into the
human psyche. As the psychologist and dreamwork pioneer
Carl Jung once wrote, "Enlightenment consists not of seeing lu-
minous lights and visions, but in making the darkness visible."

We're here to discover our own depths, and thereby to understand life itself. To do so, we need to see and acknowledge
our shadow as well as our light. As author Stephen Levine has
written, "Mindfulness teaches us the nature of the shadow;
heartfulness teaches us the nature of the light. But without these
two qualities in balance, we will evolve either eyeless in the
darkness, or blinded by the light."

Socrates undermined the illusions upon which I had based my
self-image, so I could directly confront my subjective mind. Just
as we have to "feel it to heal it," so we have to "see it to free it."

Attachment and Suffering

*"If you don't get what you want, you suffer; if you get what you
don't want, you suffer; even when you get exactly what you want,
you still suffer because you can't hold on to it forever. Your mind
is your predicament. It wants to be free of change, free of pain, free
of the obligations of life and death. But change is a law, and no
amount of pretending will alter that reality."*

*"Socrates, you can really be depressing, you know that? If life
is nothing but suffering, then why bother at all?"*

"Life is not suffering; it's just that you will suffer it, rather than enjoy it, until you let go of your mind's attachments and just go for the ride."

Georges Gurdjieff, an Armenian-born mystic, once said, "Man will give up any pleasure, but he will not relinquish his suffering." Gurdjieff shared the idea that out of a fundamental fear we cling to the familiar and wish to avoid change. When things are bad, we want them to change, at least some of the time — but even then, some of us have remained in painful or abusive situations because they were at least familiar. As the saying goes, "The devil we know is preferable to the devil we don't know."

Most explorers of uncharted territory have found themselves stuck between who they were and who they were becoming. The willingness to risk is part of the journey — not foolish risks of bravado, but existential or emotional risks — facing the great fear and finding the willingness to let go of who we think we are. Thus, choosing to live as a peaceful warrior demands and develops qualities of courage, devotion, and endurance.

As St. Augustine wrote, "Pray not for a lighter burden, but for stronger shoulders."

The Illusion Called Mind

"'Mind' is one of those slippery terms like 'love.' The proper definition depends on your state of consciousness. Look at it this way: You have a brain that directs the body, stores information, and plays with that information. We refer to the brain's abstract processes as 'the intellect.' Nowhere have I mentioned mind. The brain and the mind are not the same. The brain is real; the mind isn't.

"'Mind' is an illusory reflection . . . all the random, uncontrolled thoughts that bubble into awareness from the subconscious.

Consciousness is not mind; awareness is not mind; attention is not mind. Mind is an obstruction, an aggravation....

"The brain can be a tool. It can recall phone numbers, solve math puzzles, or create poetry. In this way, it works for the rest of the body, like a tractor. But when you can't stop thinking of that math problem or phone number, or when troubling thoughts and memories arise without your intent, it's not your brain working, but your mind wandering...the tractor has run wild."

Whether or not we agree with Soc's description of "the problem of mind," most of us experience moments when we would like to calm the thought storms that bring worries, regrets, and anxieties. Some of us have tried meditation, yoga, or other methods to reach deeper states of quiet and relaxation.

Over time, I've gained further insight into the so-called problem of random thoughts passing through our awareness. Sometimes, pleasant thoughts arise — nostalgic reveries, fantasies, and happy or peaceful images. Most often, however, the mind stuff appears in the form of problems, concerns, and unfinished business.

We seek relief from mental or emotional pain as we might seek relief from physical pain. Therapists and other mental and emotional healers serve as cognitive chiropractors, helping us to make adjustments in our ways of viewing the world.

I have made peace with my mind, whether it's filled with positive or negative thoughts. Mental activity is as natural as a bubbling hot spring. The important thing is to avoid mistaking our thoughts for reality. We don't have to change them or give them power over our lives.

As I came to realize that I have more control over what I do than over what I think or feel, I understood what Socrates was telling me — not how to fix my insides, but how to rise above the ever-changing weather of mind and emotions. Now I focus on my actions and let the rest be.

The Law of Surrender

"The rain was a perfectly lawful display of nature. Your 'upset' at the ruined picnic and your 'happiness' when the sun reappeared were the product of your thoughts. They had nothing to do with the actual events. Haven't you been 'unhappy' at celebrations for example? It is obvious then that your mind, not other people or your surroundings, is the source of your moods."

Soc's comments on our rained-out picnic began my instruction in another one of the House Rules, or spiritual laws: the principle of acceptance, or surrender, which reminds us that *stress happens when the mind resists what is.* Aligning ourselves with this law does not require that we abandon all preferences — it's natural to prefer pleasure over pain, for example — though imagine what our lives might feel like if we could just relax our preferences and learn to make the best of whatever arises in a gracious manner, with an attitude of nonresistance. As the Greek sage Epictetus said, "Learn to wish that everything should come to pass exactly as it does."

When we develop the ability to go with the flow, and flow with the moment, we experience less stress and psychological turmoil. This ability doesn't develop overnight but matures through life experience and expanding perspectives as we learn to find value in adversity.

Life unfolds as it will; making the best of it is an acquired skill. Beginners in the martial arts tend to resist a force, but masters go with the force and use it to their advantage. This is also a warrior's approach to life.

Dark Night of the Soul

I decided to try and take up the normal life I'd tossed aside months ago. . . .

My life became an ordeal. Other people's laughter hurt my ears. I imagined Socrates and Joy, cackling like warlock and witch, plotting against me. The movies I sat through had lost their colors; the food I ate tasted like paste. . . .

I'd begun to drift through the routine of school like a phantom. My world was turning inside out and upside down. I had tried to rejoin the old ways I knew, to motivate myself in my studies and training, but nothing made sense anymore.

Meanwhile, professors rattled on and on about the Renaissance, the instincts of the rat, and Milton's middle years.

Socrates once said, "I call myself a peaceful warrior because the important battles are inside." Now I faced my own inner battle — a time of disillusionment, cynicism, and mental paralysis. I felt frozen in place, stuck between two worlds, belonging fully to neither. I wanted to go back, but I had seen too much to do so; yet I couldn't see a way to go forward.

As my psyche went through this process of reorganization, I experienced a time of profound disorientation and suffering, not unlike that of those suffering from mental illness. This was my dark night of the soul, as various spiritual traditions have called it. The dark night of the soul can be a lonely time. We may find it difficult to communicate with others. Our lives may look relatively normal or even pleasant from the outside but feel very different on the inside.

If we face our dark nights squarely, however, making it through such experiences can lead to greater light and a newfound sense of compassion. Important lessons emerge from the trials and testing. I learned, for one thing, that there's a natural phase in our spiritual growth involving almost obsessive self-focus — self-remembering, self-observation, self-reflection. We have to know the self before we can transcend it.

Self-focus is a necessary phase up the mountain path of personal evolution — similar to passing through a dense forest on the way to higher altitudes. But we don't want to get lost in the shadows. Chronic self-preoccupation leads to dissatisfaction. So while this study of the self is a necessary and useful stage, it's at best a temporary one.

Once we have developed the capacity to see ourselves realistically through objective self-observation, it's time to turn our attention outward. As Japanese psychiatrist Shoma Morita once said, "When passing by a mirror, notice the frame."

We humans are sometimes like children determined to sleep when someone is shaking us, crying out, "Wake up!" Indeed, we tend to glorify those who promise us riches, success, and every sort of good feeling, but resent true awakeners so much that at times we even crucify them.

When I was first getting to know Socrates, my resistance and rigid investment in my identity generated a dark-night struggle with myself, a common marker on the path of awakening. But despite my resistance and fear, Socrates managed to keep me around long enough to pull off the blinders of self-image and self-deception. As I passed though that period of disillusionment and despair, I found the clarity and freedom on the far side of the tunnel that makes the ordeal more than worthwhile.

This ordeal is by no means inevitable. Those willing to let go of resistance can, through faith and surrender, awaken spontaneously and gracefully, in unexpected ways. For the Buddha, sitting under a bodhi tree led to such an awakening. Insights and awakenings can happen anywhere, anytime we open our hearts without conditions. We can be reborn in an instant. May it be so!

Working on Self, Working on Society

I walked through Sproul Plaza each day amid campus demonstrations and walked through sit-ins as if in a dream; none of it meant anything to me. Student power gave me no comfort.... So I drifted, a stranger in a strange land, caught between two worlds without a handhold on either.

Despite the fact that the story I tell in *Way of the Peaceful Warrior* took place during the Vietnam War and political upheavals at U.C. Berkeley, my writing barely touched upon the larger events of that era. In fact, the paragraph I've excerpted here may be the only time I even referred to political demonstrations. Some politically minded, socially conscious readers have inquired about this apparent omission.

Like my peers, I experienced all the tumult and righteous anger of the activist, idealistic youth of that time and place. "Down with the establishment! Smash the state! Make love, not war! Turn on, tune in, drop out!" But I had not set out to write a historical period piece or political commentary. My aim was to relate a more intimate story of spiritual transformation, the revolution in one young man's heart, mirrored in countless hearts and minds of every era and culture. I was more concerned with the timeless than the timely.

Albert Einstein once observed, "Problems cannot be solved at the same level of thinking which created them." So a mass awakening may be the only kind of revolution that can change the hearts, values, and priorities of our world.

Here's a sanity test: We're shown a sink with a plug in the drain and water overflowing onto the floor. Nearby we see a mop and bucket. Our sanity is measured by our choice: Do we grab the mop and start mopping, or do we first turn off the water and unplug the drain? Every era has its turmoil and suffering; the realm of politics is a necessary form of mopping up.

In the global arena of politics and nations, many high-minded, intelligent, well-intentioned, and hardworking women and men do their best to compromise between interest groups and conflicting ideologies tinged by fear, self-interest, and competition. As perennial presidential candidate Eugene McCarthy once said, "Being in politics is like being a football coach: You have to be smart enough to understand the game, and dumb enough to think it's important."

A spiritual change in the hearts of human beings, such as that related in *Way of the Peaceful Warrior*, may finally enable us to see ourselves as one human family and serve to pull the plug and stem the tides of flowing blood that still plague our planet.

This is why the book did not concern itself with the current events of the 1960s, or with the war of ideas and ever-changing public dramas, but rather addressed the battles within and our universal search for illumination.

I applaud those who seek social and political solutions to the problems that arise in our evolving world. But even as social activists and public servants pursue their calling, I speak of a path of personal transformation that can also contribute toward a more peaceful and loving world.

To Be or Not to Be?

Late one afternoon I sat in a redwood grove near the bottom of campus, waiting for the darkness, thinking about the best way to kill myself.

There are times in our lives when some of us must confront the existential question posed by William Shakespeare's young Hamlet:

To be, or not to be: that is the question:
Whether 'tis nobler in the mind to suffer
The slings and arrows of outrageous fortune,
Or to take arms against a sea of troubles,
And by opposing end them? To die: to sleep;
No more; and by a sleep to say we end
The heart-ache and the thousand natural shocks
That flesh is heir to, 'tis a consummation
Devoutly to be wish'd. To die, to sleep;
To sleep: perchance to dream: ay, there's the rub;
 For in that sleep of death what dreams may come...

During this period, I wandered through campus like a home-
less man — unshaven, unkempt, alienated, lost between my past
and future, between the comfort of conventional life and the
frightening unknown of what Socrates seemed to offer.

In this state of psychological paralysis and suffering, I was
forced to confront questions about meaning, life, and death. As
I stood on this inner precipice, I came face-to-face with the core
of my life, my identity, my existence. While I was not ready to
step off the brink into suicide, I could empathize with others
staring into that abyss, as the abyss called out to them. I wrote
about this period as a way of reaching out to others on the
brink, to say: You are a story in the making, and no one can pre-
dict what the next chapter, the next day, the next moment, will
bring. No matter how dark it may seem, whatever the pain or
emptiness we may feel — the sense of despair, the loss of hope
or meaning — our dark night will be followed by a new dawn
if we just endure. So take no desperate action; face the fear. Let
the ego die, but protect the body. Allow this "death" to become
a rebirth. And as day follows night, the dark tunnel will lead to a
greater light.

A New Way of Living

"You don't have to do anything except to stop seeing the world from the viewpoint of your own personal cravings. Loosen up! When you lose your mind, you'll come to your senses."

By "lose your mind," Socrates was not referring to going insane or becoming irrational. On the contrary, he was talking about *paying attention* to the reality around me, rather than merely thinking about it. He served to remove the veil of thought that interfered with my direct perception. Over time, as my awareness focused on the world around me, I began to feel the temperature of the air on my skin, smell aromas carried on the breeze, notice the sights and sounds in this multimedia realm we call daily life.

Soc pulled me out of my subjective mental existence — my preoccupations and attachments to every passing thought, impulse, or emotion — into a spacious sensory world. In letting go of the smaller self, I awoke to a larger life.

CUTTING FREE

*I discovered the secret of the sea
in meditation upon a dewdrop.*

—— KAHLIL GIBRAN

Paying Attention

*Later that morning, I went running around Edwards Field. There I
met Dwight, who worked up at the Lawrence Hall of Science in
the Berkeley hills. I had to ask his name a second time, because I
"didn't catch it" the first time, another reminder of my lack of attention and wandering mind. After a few laps, Dwight remarked
about the cloudless blue sky. But lost in thought, I hadn't even noticed the sky. Then he headed for the hills —— he was a marathon
runner —— and I returned home, thinking about my mind —— a self-
defeating activity if ever there was one.*

In this phase of my training, Socrates deepened my insight into the mind's interference with a clear and direct perception of reality. I began to grasp the degree of my preoccupation with the contents of my mind. I hardly noticed what was going on around me. I didn't catch people's names and missed other details about my surroundings. Unless I was forced to concentrate while flying through the air or swinging around the bars, I paid more attention to my thoughts *about* the world than to the world itself.

How many of us have driven for a mile or two down the highway and suddenly realized we were so lost in thought that we didn't even notice the past few miles? Or that we had missed our exit? (A sobering thought, when you consider how many distracted, preoccupied, absentminded people are out on the road.)

We humans are lenses that focus awareness into what we call attention. We direct that attention wherever we choose — or left to its own devices, it wanders inside and out like a child sleepwalking through a dream. One moment we pay attention to eating a bite of food; the next instant someone nearby laughs, and we're no longer tasting our food. Then our attention is captured by a thought for a few moments more before we sigh and look once again at our plate, now empty. And so it goes, this wandering play of attention.

We're always paying attention — to something. The question is, moment to moment, what are we paying attention to — inside or out, the mud or the stars?

Mind Ripples

"For example, you have a cold now; its physical symptoms tell you when your body needs to rebalance itself, to restore its proper relationship with sunlight, fresh air, simple food. Just so, stressful

thoughts reflect a conflict with reality. Stress happens when the mind resists what is. . . .

"When you understand the source, you'll see that the ripples of your mind have nothing to do with you; you'll just watch them, without attachment, no longer compelled to overreact every time a pebble drops. You will be free of the world's turbulence as soon as you stop taking your thoughts so seriously."

One of the lessons most difficult for me to grasp was that my emotional and mental suffering came not so much from what was happening, but from my thoughts *about* what was happening. As Mark Twain wrote, "I've had many troubles in my life, most of which never happened."

Even physical pain is influenced by thought and stress. When the body hurts but we're paying attention to what is going on around us in the present moment, not thinking about when the pain started, or how long it may last, or what it all means — when it's only pain, without extras or complications — we suffer less. (Pain without fear or tension is far less intense than pain plus fear.)

Mental and emotional suffering stems from resistance — and attachment to beliefs about what should or shouldn't be. The first step to liberation is to resign as general manager of the universe and embrace the advice of writer Isaac Bashevis Singer: "Life is God's novel; let God write it."

I no longer presume to know how life should come or go; letting go in this way brings a sense of freedom. This doesn't mean I don't care or have no preferences. My actions naturally follow the call of my heart, my interests, my values. I make efforts in my personal and professional life in alignment with my goals. But once I've taken aim and loosed the arrow from the bow, I can only wait with interest to see where it will land.

The Silent Sword

"Silence is the warrior's art — and meditation is his sword....

"With it, he cuts the mind to ribbons, slashing through thoughts to reveal their lack of substance."

Once viewed as a religious ritual from the East, the practice of meditation has now garnered widespread acceptance in the West. Many books and teachers have emerged promoting traditions from India, China, and Japan. Various methods of meditation have drawn hundreds of thousands of new practitioners. And many engage in the Buddhist practice of *zazen*, or "just sitting." Reasearchers have cited numerous benefits of this ancient practice.

Yet some seekers place meditation on a pedestal, lauding it as the key to reaching enlightenment, and many misconceptions remain about to how to meditate and what results to expect.

Socrates had studied a global array of practices and discovered that there is no single best approach for everyone — only an appropriate practice for each individual at a given stage in life.

As with any activity, such as doing push-ups or playing the violin, we improve with practice over time. But progress in this inner art of meditation is more difficult to measure; when we sit and close our eyes, it's all too easy to daydream. I'm a big fan of daydreaming, but I don't confuse it with meditation practice, which involves a commitment to release all that arises in the field of awareness — to sit on the shore and watch it all float past rather than drifting downstream with it.

Such meditation practice doesn't necessarily lead *to* enlightenment but rather is in itself the practice *of* enlightenment: As we sit with spine erect — not leaning forward into the future or backward into the past — relaxing the body, watching the natural cycles of breathing, as thoughts, feelings, and sensations arise, we maintain the posture and disposition of the witness — a pure, detached, transcendent awareness, observing all, allowing all, clinging to nothing, until we realize that we are the awareness that exists beyond the body, mind, or identity.

The process itself   taking time out from this passing world — is its own reward. As we allow our attention to rest, effortlessly, on the breath, or on a mantra or other inner sound or image, the mind *seems* to quiet, and time passes quickly as our attention rests in a timeless place of absorption, referred to as *samadhi* in some traditions, *satori* in others.

Once we open our eyes and get on with the day, thoughts continue to arise. The point of the practice is not to get rid of thoughts but to make peace with them, to realize their lack of substance. Once we see the nature of mind, the practice is no longer necessary, except as a pleasurable respite from the business of the world — an inner retreat, a form of Sabbath, rest, and refreshment.

The world is far more interesting than our thoughts about it. Looking inward has benefits, but so does looking outward. The peaceful warrior's way involves the ability to do both with full attention, so that the world around us also becomes an object of meditation.

Spiritual Progress

After the car sped away we remained at the pump, smelling the night air. "You treated these people so courteously but were positively obnoxious to our blue-robed seekers, who were obviously on a higher evolutionary level. What's the story?"

For once, he gave me a simple, direct answer. "The only levels that should concern you are mine — and yours," he said with a grin. "These people needed kindness. The spiritual seekers needed something else to reflect upon."

Socrates had developed the ability to discern and give people what they most needed, but not necessarily what they wanted. Some of us need, at a given time, simple human kindness, respect, courtesy. Others, like myself, occasionally need tough love.

The outward appearance or trappings of spirituality are little more than a fashion statement. No matter what we wear or where we live, our behavior remains the most reliable indicator of our state of spiritual maturity. We may understand the domains of consciousness or other esoteric models or concepts, but the real questions remain: Can we show kindness and compassion even when we're not feeling like it? Do we behave in a constructive, positive, and functional manner? Do we live balanced lives that include moderate exercise, balanced diets, and sufficient rest? Do we approach all our activities (raising children, working, playing, gardening) with quality, as paths of service and growth?

How we live and what we do, moment to moment, tells our story. It has always been so. That's why Mahatma Gandhi said, "My life is my teaching." This was also true of Socrates, and I hope it's true of me.

Maps and Lightbulbs

"What you need is a map of the entire terrain you need to explore. Then you'll realize the uses, and the limits, of meditation. And I ask you, where can you get a good map?"

"At a service station, of course."

Socrates had more metaphors to offer than brands of motor oil. Part of what he offered me, and what I've offered in my books over the past twenty-five years, are maps to the territory of every-day life.

If our lives are a journey up a mountain, we travel by many different paths to the summit; each of us chooses our own route and pace. Those who have walked ahead, and have sometimes stumbled or fallen only to rise again, may offer useful guidance — a map of the way.

That's what Soc offered me, and what I offer as well. I'm not alone by any means. Each of us can share the wisdom of our experience. There's a saying in the martial arts: "Learn one day's worth; teach one day's worth." The masters on the moun-taintop may be less useful to us than those close enough to reach back and offer helping hands or kind words. And we can offer the same for those who follow.

The Visionary Path of Mystical Experience

For an instant, from a vantage point somewhere in space, I felt my-self expanding at the speed of light, ballooning, exploding to the outermost limits of existence until I was the universe. Nothing sep-arate remained. I had become everything. I was Consciousness, rec-ognizing itself; I was the pure light that physicists equate with all matter, and poets define as love. I was one, and I was all. . . .

In a flash, I was back in my mortal form, floating among the stars. I saw a prism shaped like a human heart, which dwarfed every galaxy. It diffracted the light of consciousness into an explosion of radiant colors, sparkling splinters of every rainbow hue, spreading throughout the cosmos.

My own body became a radiant prism, throwing splinters of multicolored light everywhere. And it came to me that the highest purpose of the human body is to become a clear channel for this light. . . .

I learned the meaning of attention — it is the intentional chan-
neling of awareness. . . . Finally, I realized the process of real medi-
tation — to expand awareness, to direct attention, to ultimately
surrender to the light of consciousness. . . .

"These little journeys do save me some difficult explanations I
must go through to enlighten you."

This was another of those inner journeys that saved Socrates
"some difficult explanations." I wrote about these inner journeys for the same purpose.

Suppose Socrates had sat me down and given me a lecture
on the nature of consciousness, awareness, attention. The words
might have been accurate, clear, even interesting, but they
wouldn't have had the same impact as direct experience for me
or for my readers.

Poetry reaches deeper than prose because it speaks the language of the subconscious and sows seeds beneath the surface
layers of the mind through metaphor, archetype, and symbol. In
the same way, the vivid imagery of visionary journeys provides
a sort of magic carpet for visiting the deep spaces of the psyche.

Paradox, Humor, and Change

He took out a small card. It looked normal enough, until I noticed a
faint glow. In embossed letters, it said,

Warrior, Inc.

Socrates, Prop.

Specializing in:

Paradox, Humor, and Change

Paradox, humor, and change — the three eternal truths on
which Socrates founded his message and teachings. These three

words summarize the state of the world, life, and the universe. From this trinity came all those House Rules, the spiritual laws Soc would refer to on occasion.

In the *Peaceful Warrior* motion picture, during a hike up into the hills, the character Dan summarizes what he understands about this trinity. But as Socrates would remind us all, *doing* is understanding.

Paradox testifies to the cosmic fact that we live in a world of apparent duality (light and darkness, good and evil) and speaks to the simultaneous existence of both. As Charles Dickens expressed in the famous opening to *A Tale of Two Cities*: "It was the best of times, it was the worst of times; it was the age of wisdom, it was the age of foolishness; it was the epoch of belief, it was the epoch of incredulity...."

Even within our psyches we can find polarized characters: the puritan and the hedonist, the believer and the doubter, the social butterfly and the lone wolf. Paradox points to such dualities of life and of the psyche — and to the mystery of our existence.

In everyday life we encounter a host of paradoxical truths: We're separate, yet we are one; accidents happen, yet there are no accidents; death is real, yet death is an illusion. Both views are valid from their respective conventional or transcendental perspective.

Even the idea of "living in the present moment" is a paradox, since the present moment doesn't actually exist! By the time I utter the word *now*, between *nnnn* and *owww* a thousand moments have come and gone. We cannot grasp the moment or seize the day; all we can do is go with the flow of time. There's no past, no future, no present — no time at all. When I speak of "staying in the present," I'm referring to focusing on what's right in front of us and not getting preoccupied with either memories or imagined futures. (The past and future may be nice places to visit, but we don't want to live there.)

The term *peaceful warrior* is itself a paradox — how can we be both at the same time? Yet when these two apparent opposites combine, they form a whole that is greater than the sum of the parts: love and courage— a peaceful heart and a warrior spirit.

Humor, in Soc's view, involves far more than jokes that provoke laughter. The humor to which he referred is divine humor, which flows from a transcendental perspective — not taking life or death, self or world, quite so seriously. When each of us is viewing the world through our own two eyes, life can seem extremely serious at times. But seen from God's eyes (or Soc's), as viewed from the infinite void of space with its billions of whirling galaxies, our problems with leaky plumbing or relationship issues come into their proper perspective, and humor is restored.

Change, as I've noted, is a law of reality. The Roman emperor and Stoic philosopher Marcus Aurelius said, "Life is a river of passing events; no sooner is one thing brought to sight than it is swept away and another takes its place, and this, too, will be swept away."

Our thoughts, feelings, and reality change moment to moment; even the cells of our bodies are constantly being renewed. Even our personalities change constantly. One moment I'm kind; another, I'm thoughtless. Even what we call "I" is not a thing but a process, a series of actions — alternately kind, silly, focused, diffused — sometimes this, sometimes that. And the world changes around us, moment to moment, day to day, year to year. People come and go, are born and die, enter and exit. We want love to last forever; we cling to possessions. But all that is mortal dies, all matter turns to dust, and we lose all that we love. As the Buddha said, "Everything that begins also ends. Make peace with that and all will be well."

As Socrates pointed out, the more we accept paradox, humor, and change, the more skillfully we ride the river of reality. So let's make peace with paradox, view the world through humorous eyes, and embrace change without resistance, like the Japanese poet Masahide, who wrote, "Now that my house has burned down, I have a better view of the rising moon."

The Mindless Body

"Meditation consists of two simultaneous processes: One is insight *— paying attention to what is arising. The other is* surrender *— letting go of attachment to arising thoughts. This is how you cut free of the mind....*

"Consciousness is not in the body; the body is in Consciousness. And you are that Consciousness — not the phantom mind that troubles you so. You are the body, but you are everything else, too. That is what your vision revealed to you. Only the mind resists change. When you relax mindless into the body, you are happy and content and free, sensing no separation."

This selection is one of the most challenging of any in *Way of the Peaceful Warrior.* You don't need to wrap your mind entirely around it; you need only acquire an intuitive feel for the perspective that you are not a mind "in" a body but rather a body without a mind, knowing no separation.

If you hold a tight fist up in the air — right now — you can feel that fist as separate from the air around it. This kind of clenching is what our psyches habitually do, creating an illusory sense of separation from others and from our environments. Thus, what we call *ego* is not a "thing," but rather a chronic action of contraction.

If you relax your hand, you no longer feel where your hand ends and space begins. Similarly, the relaxed bodymind is connected to, and at one with, its environment — with the air, with all that is happening "inside" and "out." Only the mind defines itself as a separate "I." That old saying "Be the ball," which many cynics make fun of, turns out to be quite good advice. Be the ball. Be the world. When author and spiritual teacher J. Krishnamurti advised listeners, "You are the world," he was speaking not just poetically but literally, from this same realization.

All the work and all the spiritual practices for purifying and balancing and opening to energy exist to let the message penetrate at last — to allow us to *realize* the truth of it.

In the last few sentences in this excerpt from *Way of the Peaceful Warrior*, Socrates laid it out for me. But it wasn't until the death and rebirth I describe at the end of the book that this realization became a living truth for me, and in a sense, perhaps even for some of my readers. Perhaps this is why many have returned to the book for a reminder about what they have always known.

After Sitting, Everyday Life

"Why should a warrior sit around meditating?" I asked. "I thought the warrior's way was about action."

"Sitting meditation is the beginner's practice. Eventually, you will learn to meditate in every action. Sitting serves as a ceremony, a time to practice balance, ease, and divine detachment. Master the ritual before you expand the same insight and surrender fully into daily life."

We've already begun to address the subject of meditation — what this ritual or practice accomplishes, and what it does not.

Here I wish to comment on the importance of ceremony. The tea ceremony of Japan, for example, serves as a meditative ritual of movement and attention, a bridge between sitting in stillness with eyes closed or half-open and meditating in everyday life. We begin with sitting. Then we learn to meditate as we walk, or serve tea, or play a sport — until we bring the same relaxed awareness, focus, and ease into advanced practices such as doing the dishes, eating a meal, making love, or folding laundry.

The practice of ceremony elevates and transmutes *doing* into art through both feeling and attention. Ceremony integrates body, mind and spirit. Normally, we experience the power of ceremony only on "special occasions," such as at weddings, christenings, bar mitzvahs, and so forth. But as Socrates was quick to demonstrate, every moment is a special occasion.

When we invest our full attention and spirits in each movement we make, going beyond rote or repetitive behavior, we transform the quality of the moment, of our psyches and our lives — until our every action becomes ceremony, and our lives serve as good examples to others.

The Meaning of Happiness

"I am completely happy, you see. Are you?"

A car pulled in, clouds of steam surrounding its radiator. "Come on," Soc said. "This car is suffering and we may have to shoot it and put it out of its misery." We both went out to the stricken car, whose radiator was boiling and whose owner was in a foul mood, fuming.

"What took you so long? I can't wait around here all night, damn it!"

Socrates looked at him with nothing less than loving compassion. "Let's see if we can't help you, sir, and make this only a minor inconvenience." He had the man drive into the garage, where he put a pressure cap on the radiator and found the leak. Within a few minutes he'd welded the hole shut but told the man that he would still need a new radiator in the near future. "Everything dies and changes, even radiators," he winked at me.

As the man drove away, the truth of Soc's words sank in. He really was completely happy! Nothing seemed to affect his happy mood. In all the time I'd known him, he had acted angry, sad, gentle, tough, humorous, and even concerned. But always, a kind of peace and happiness had shone in his eyes, even when they brimmed with tears.

When Socrates spoke of happiness, he was referring to a different sort of state than the passing emotion that we normally refer to as "feeling good." He was talking about a warrior spirit — radiating positive energy and light into the world even as surface emotions rise and pass. This distinction is central to the entire book and to the peaceful warrior's way: Socrates never believed, nor have I, that the end point of human evolution is walking around with self-satisfied, gleeful smiles on our faces.

Anyone can claim to be happy — how can we know if it's true? Is there a difference between *feeling* happy and *acting* happy? And which is more controllable — feeling happy or behaving as if we were? (Please consider this carefully before responding.) And here's another question worth pondering: Would you rather live with an enlightened person who acted crazy, or a crazy person who acted enlightened?

Of course feeling happy is a pleasurable state, but that feeling is not under our direct control or we could simply will ourselves to feel happy in any moment. We cannot do that, but we can will ourselves to smile, to laugh, to act *as if* we're happy, even when we're feeling bored or melancholy.

It isn't that we should ignore or deny our feelings. Chronic depression or any other negative emotion may indicate that we need to visit a helping professional and make constructive changes in our lives. But even as we honor and learn from our emotions, positive or negative, we can take on the peaceful warrior practice of behaving as if we were (feeling) happy, courageous, and kind.

At this point in my life, I experience a sort of underlying happiness/okayness even as I feel the normal emotional ups and downs of life. And many of us have felt melancholy and happy at the same time — an example of the paradoxical nature of emotions.

If we persist in trying to "feel better about ourselves" while assuming that we're these temporary little personalities walking around solving problems all day, we're not likely to feel happy except during momentary incidents of pleasure or satisfaction, when we hear good news or get what we want. But such feel-good moments are fleeting, and soon we're off seeking the next one.

It has become clear to me — and it took sixty years and a great deal of experience to reach even this tentative conclusion — that what we truly seek is meaning, purpose, and connection; we seek the transcendent. And the only way to experience this unconditional bliss is to have realized our divine source and nature — to experience complete liberation from the separate self.

Socrates had realized the transcendent secret of our existence, so that even in moments of sorrow or pain or loss, or when facing his own death, he knew who he was: that eternal awareness that transcends all play, all appearances, all limitations. He was free and happy, even while changing the oil of an old pickup truck or trying to instill some sense into a naive and self-important young athlete.

That is what Soc meant when he asked me if I was completely happy. He forced me to confront the reality beneath my confident surface: Despite all my achievements and youth, I felt empty and afraid and confused. He had something I wanted. And that something kept me around when the going got tough.

ON BOOK TWO

THE WARRIOR'S TRAINING

You can map out a fight plan or a life plan,
but when the action starts,
it may not go the way you planned,
and you're down to the reflexes
you developed in training.
That's where roadwork shows —
the training you did in the dark of the mornin'
will show when you're under the bright lights.

— JOE FRAZIER

THE SWORD IS SHARPENED

As soon as one cherishes the thought
of winning the contest or displaying
one's skill and technique,
swordsmanship is doomed.

— TAKANO SHIGEYOSHI

Good Luck, Bad Luck

Joy gently turned my face to hers and looked into my eyes. "Socrates has a message for you, Danny; he asked me to tell you this story."

I closed my eyes and listened intently.

An old man and his son worked a small farm, with only one horse to pull the plow. One day, the horse ran away.

"How terrible," sympathized the neighbors. "What bad luck."

"Who knows whether it is bad luck or good luck," the farmer replied.

A week later, the horse returned from the mountains, leading five wild mares into the barn.

"What wonderful luck!" said the neighbors.

"Good luck? Bad luck? Who knows?" answered the old man.

The next day, the son, trying to tame one of the horses, fell and broke his leg.

"How terrible. What bad luck!"

"Bad luck? Good luck?"

The army came to all the farms to take the young men for war, but the farmer's son was of no use to them, so he was spared.

"Good? Bad?"

This story — a favorite for many readers of *Way of the Peaceful Warrior* — came from Joy, as she sat on my hospital bed after the injury that was to challenge and change my life.

Her point then, and mine now: When we cease presuming to know what is ultimately good or bad and instead abide in faith — when we meet each moment without judgment or expectation — we live in a different way. Knowers are an uptight breed, clinging to how things ought to be, solving problems, struggling to make everything come out "right."

What would happen if we made no more assumptions about what it all means or how things should work out, and just let life unfold, making the best of each new wave of pleasure or pain, success or failure — all part of the texture of life? Because what has happened to us, no matter how welcome or tragic or unfair, should have happened because it did happen, and nothing can change that.

Acceptance is one of the universal laws of life — the most creative, assertive, and intelligent response we can make to any moment or experience. It turns out that the Borg on *Star Trek* were right: Resistance *is* futile. (And exhausting!)

When I was teaching children's gymnastics, the little ones would often push and shove one another to be first in line. Instead of repeatedly asking them not to shove or push to be first, I'd wait for them to get in line; then I'd walk to the back of the line and declare that the last in line was first. After that, they ceased pushing for position. They stopped being knowers and started waiting to see what would happen. A good policy for life.

The flat tire when we're late to an important meeting may end up saving us from a fatal accident at the next intersection — or may set us up for one. The point is, *we do not know*. Understanding this, we stop trying to play God.

Our struggles provide the best times of learning. Faith is the courage to live as if everything that happens is for our highest good and learning. So whenever we resist reality or face challenges, we can remind ourselves: "Good luck? Bad luck? Who knows?" This perspective can help us to relax more into life, into faith, into mystery. Because we simply do not know.

Clean Living

In the past I had noticed a light that seemed to encircle him, but I'd assumed it was only my tired eyes. I wasn't tired now, and there was no doubt about it — it was a barely perceptible aura. "Socrates," I said, "there's a light shining around your body. Where does it come from?"

"Clean living."

Many of us have noticed that some people seem to have a healthy glow about them. They radiate energy; we may detect a rarified field around them, a certain feeling we get around them. Maybe it's our imagination, maybe it's their personalities or charisma, or maybe it's something else.

We all glow with happiness at times, or with enthusiasm. Our expressions change, along with our breathing and our gestures. Maybe we stand up straighter. Could it be that the energy fields around us also change? While I don't often use the word *aura*, it stands to reason that just as the earth is surrounded by an electromagnetic field and an atmosphere, every living being is surrounded by a bioenergetic field.

Some people claim that they can detect or even see such energy fields, and they attribute colors to them — and meanings to the colors. Even those of us who are not so gifted or sensitive or imaginative can sometimes sense people's energy fields as lighter, darker, or heavier. And no one radiates the same kind of energy all the time (just as we're not in the same mood all the time).

Those who have read my book *The Life You Were Born to Live* may remember that certain people — whether because of genetics or karma or frequency — have a lot of potential creative energy circulating through them. But energy is a double-edged sword: In the positive, such people have a lot of "juice" — animals love to get petted by these folks, and plants often thrive under their care. But they sometimes don't know what to do with all their energy, so they may employ various means (some constructive, such as exercise; some destructive, such as using alcohol, tobacco, or other drugs) to release the energetic pressure they experience as tension or discomfort. (I've covered this topic in the chapter "Universal Addictions" in another one of my books, *No Ordinary Moments*.)

Paying attention to the energetic world in and around us can provide an interesting field of exploration. The primary thing is to acknowledge the energy we have, maintain the flow, and spend it wisely. We don't really have to eat special substances or do anything unusual to get more energy from the outside, since we take in energy with every conscious breath, filling ourselves not only with oxygen and other gases but with light. We get energy from the friends around us, from the food we eat, from the sun and the natural world. The main thing is not to squander our energy.

There's a story you may have heard about a man who spent most of his life searching for more light, energy, and spirit. After many years, he sensed that his long quest had ended when he came upon a sacred mountain, piercing the clouds. After a long and arduous ascent to the top, he spread his arms and cried up to the heavens, "Fill me full of light, energy, and spirit!"

The clouds parted and a voice thundered down, "I'm *always* filling you, but you keep leaking!"

Through breath and relaxation, we can consciously fill our bodies with the light of awareness. We can also reduce the leaks of unnecessary tension, fidgeting, and idle chatter, and allow more energy (which some call *prana*, *chi*, or *ki*) to circulate in and around us. Then we, like Socrates, may exude a certain glow.

The Realm of the Warrior

"The realm of the warrior is guarded by something like a gate.... Many knock, but few enter."

If we lie down in a quiet location and put our thumbs over our eardrums, we'll hear only silence at first; in that silence, our awareness begins to fine-tune. After a few seconds or a few minutes, we hear a high-pitched tone at the edge of our awareness. We may realize that it has always been there, and that it's natural to us. We can meditate on that inner sound, using it as an object of attention. With time we may hear more subtle sounds — up to twelve different tones, each more refined than the last, drawing attention into deeper places.

The sounds are always with us, but few of us have the free attention to notice. This attunement requires practice. Similarly, "the realm of the warrior" to which Socrates refers in this passage is not somewhere else, in a different dimension of time or space, or in a parallel universe. This realm is right in front of us, here and now — in this world, this life, this moment.

There's no physical gate we have to find, in some shamanic netherworld, to enter the realm of the warrior — although such images make for good fiction and fascinating imagery. The "warrior's gate" is a metaphor about our daily lives — the arena of our training — in which we eventually pass through not one gate but twelve (see my book *Everyday Enlightenment: The Twelve Gateways to Personal Growth*).

The realm of the peaceful warrior is open to all, and all of us find these gateways along the path. Passage requires heart, courage, clarity, energy, and attention. As the Buddhist patriarch Bodhidharma, said, "All know the way, but few walk it."

This *way* to which I refer is open to all — not some private club based on status, popularity, wealth, or academic degrees. There are no colored belts to earn, nor is there one dramatic initiation; rather, there are many — all provided perfectly, within the context of our everyday lives. This universal path reveals itself in each passing moment, wherein we behave as peaceful warriors — or we don't.

In some moments, I'm more of a peaceful warrior; in other moments, less. The same is true for anyone. The great challenge of each day is to increase our moments of courage and kindness.

House Rules, Universal Laws

"To find the gate, you'll have to follow —"
"The House Rules?" I interrupted.

The term *House Rules* comes from poker, or more broadly, from games of chance, like Life. Whoever represents the "house" makes the particular rules. Although he once expressed a certain fondness for poker, Socrates was referring to *universal laws, natural laws, spiritual laws* (terms I use interchangeably and address more fully in *The Laws of Spirit*).

The House Rules are as real and consistent as the law of gravity, one example of a universal law operating in the physical domain. Other laws describe how flowers turn to the sun or determine the shape of waves breaking on the shore. These laws, taken together, are human formulations of the operating principles of the universe, the earth, and our interactions.

Both scientists (representing *logos*, reason, the left brain) and mystics (representing *mythos*, intuition, the right brain) seek to understand these laws. But they use different methods of investigation.

Spiritual laws describe how life works — they are the laws of reality. Reality is based not on our concepts of right and wrong but rather on action and consequences. In other words, if I ignore the law of gravity while mountain climbing or skydiving, such ignorance doesn't make me a bad person, but it may have fatal consequences.

When we finally accept the dominion of the House Rules, life works better — we no longer suffer from the illusion that we can ignore or bend or break the laws of spirit, or avoid the consequences of our actions.

So when Socrates responded to one of my questions with a shrug and a reference to the House Rules (which I address in *Living on Purpose*), he was directing my attention to the laws of reality upon which the peaceful warrior's way is founded.

Approaches to Healing

My head felt feverish, and I ached all over. I leaned against the desk again. Out of the corner of my eye I saw Socrates come toward me, reaching out for my head. Oh no, not now; I'm not up to it, I thought. But he was only feeling my clammy forehead. Then he checked the glands in my neck, looked at my face and eyes, and felt my pulse. . . .

Then he took a small bottle of yellow liquid in which were floating more crushed herbs, and massaged the liquid deep into my right leg, directly over the scar. . . .

"What is that yellow stuff in the bottle, Soc?"

"Urine, with a few herbs."

"Urine!" I said, pulling my leg away from him in disgust.

"Don't be silly," he said, grabbing my leg and pulling it back. "Urine is a respected elixir in the ancient healing traditions."

In my college days I did come down with a case of mononucleosis, which used to be known as the "kissing disease" due to a popular means of transmission. My spleen was swollen and my throat sore, and I ended up spending a few days in the student health center. The diagnosis and treatment consisted of conventional medicine and good advice about resting and taking care of my body and immune system. Several weeks and many afternoon naps later, I was back in shape.

Only later did I experiment with ancient healing practices, including the medicinal uses of herbs and even urine. I recall the advice my public health professor at Berkeley gave the class: If we were stuck in the woods and had an open wound, such as a minor cut, it would be wiser to pee on it rather than "kiss it and make it better," since saliva has innumerable bacteria, but *fresh* urine has antiseptic properties. The ancient Ayurvedic tradition of India might prescribe use of your own fresh urine as an elixir, gargled for sore throats and so forth. However, since bacteria form quickly in urine, it isn't used or generally recommended in modern medicine (although another ancient practice, the use of leeches, has made a comeback in some circumstances).

Many of us who gravitate toward ancient or "natural" forms of healing may look on modern medicine with suspicion, while placing alternative (or complementary) medicine on a pedestal, favoring herbs over "drugs." Yet some modern drugs are relatively benign in their side effects and can be quite helpful, even lifesaving, while certain herbs in the wrong dosages or combinations can be harmful, even deadly.

The best physicians I know strive to use whatever means, ancient or modern, that have been tested and found to be effective. In any case, it seems wise to take a rational approach to helping the body heal itself, whether by using conventional modern treatments or applying ancient remedies. Modern medicine has made great strides over the centuries, yet we continue to gain insight and wisdom about the use or misuse of the various approaches to health and healing.

My primary point here is not to encourage anyone to adopt the exact dietary recommendations or other methods Socrates used in treating me, but to show how he opened my mind to new approaches to healing and to life.

Emotion and Action

"Nothing wrong with anger or any other emotion. Just pay attention to how you behave....Anger is a powerful tool to transform old habits...and replace them with new ones....Fear and sorrow inhibit action; anger generates it. When you learn to make proper use of your anger, you can change fear and sorrow to anger, then turn anger to action. That's the body's secret of internal alchemy."...

"How can I control my habits if I can't even seem to control my emotions?"

"You don't need to control emotion," he said. "Emotions are natural, like passing weather. The key is to transform the energy of emotion into constructive action."

A man I once counseled told me he suffered from bouts of rage and wanted to know how he could "stop getting so angry." I suggested that it might be more useful to address his behavior rather than his anger. The problem was not his rage; it was how he behaved when he felt that rage.

We humans tend to live a soap-opera existence, letting our emotions run the show. (To see examples of emotion-centered lives, turn on a television soap opera — or simply watch your relatives.) Believing that we have emotional problems, we seek ways to experience more positive emotions (like confidence and courage and compassion and motivation and passion) and to rid ourselves of so-called negative emotions (like fear and sorrow and anger) so that we can live well and behave better and accomplish more.

We hope that the next motivational speaker or self-help text or counselor can help us to focus on and find techniques or perspectives to manage our emotions. But we do not need to change our emotions; they are fine and natural as they are. *We need to change our behavior.*

There are two basic methods to effect this change. Method One is quite popular: We quiet our minds and create empowering beliefs, practice positive self-talk, sharpen our focus, and affirm our power in order to free our emotions and visualize positive outcomes to develop confidence and generate the courage to find the determination to make the commitment to feel sufficiently motivated to do whatever it is we need to do.

Method Two reflects the warrior's way: We just do it.

In a more ideal world populated by saints, everyone would immediately opt for the second method. But in the real world, few people will "just quit" an addictive substance, or "simply exercise more and eat less" to lose weight. Many of us need a period of time and a step-by-step process to adapt to a new way of living. Group support, appropriate programs, and therapeutic processes can serve as transitions to finally "just doing it." The caterpillar doesn't become a butterfly overnight. Some transformations take a little time.

So let's be gentle with ourselves as we turn knowing into doing, and as we learn to use our emotions (instead of the other way around). As Mahatma Gandhi said, "As heat conserved becomes energy, our anger can become a power which can move the world."

Dietary Intelligence

"No one is a warrior like me," he answered, laughing. "Nor would anyone want to be. Each of us has natural qualities. For example, while you've excelled in gymnastics, Joseph has mastered the preparation of food....

"You'll need to refine every human function — moving, sleeping, breathing, thinking, feeling — and eating. Of all the human activities, eating is one of the most important to stabilize first."...

"How is changing a few things in my diet going to make a difference?"

"Your present diet...makes you groggy, affects your moods, and lowers your level of awareness....

"I eat only what is wholesome, and I eat only as much as I need. In order to appreciate what you call 'natural' foods, you have to sharpen your instincts; you have to become a natural man....

"My diet may at first seem spartan compared to the indulgences you call 'moderation,' Dan, but I take great pleasure in what I eat because I've developed the capacity to enjoy the simplest foods. And so will you."

This phase of my training with Socrates — and this section of *Way of the Peaceful Warrior* — addressed a new approach to "rational discipline": understanding and changing habits, and learning to do what needed to be done whether or not I was in the mood.

None of us exploring higher ways of life can bypass the fundamental area of the food we put in our bodies. So my old mentor introduced me to a more refined, lighter diet. Many readers took his recommendations for me as some sort of universal dietary system. But it isn't necessary to fast, or to become a vegetarian or vegan, or to eat only raw foods in order to adapt to a higher way of life (although supporters of these various approaches may disagree with me).

Still, addressing this most fundamental area of life — to find out what sort of diet works best for each of us — is a necessary part of the warrior's path. Whatever our choices, we need to be conscious of what we eat, how and how much we eat, and when we eat. Right eating, like right breathing, posture, and speaking — needs to be addressed as we adapt our bodymind to a fuller, deeper way of living.

I'm not about to suggest a particular philosophy or method; no one formula fits all. While we share the realities of human bodies and digestive systems, we also have individual differences: Some of us naturally eat at a faster or slower pace than others; some of us chew our food thoroughly, others less so. Some of us who come from certain cultural, regional, or genetic backgrounds have an easier or harder time digesting various foods.

Joseph, one of Soc's former students and friends, excelled in preparing raw foods, and his meals were delicious! It was his art, but not his religion. Joseph once told me, "Eat more of what is good for you and less of what is not. Experiment; pay attention; and find out what works for you." I can give no better advice.

Some lighter, purifying, rejuvenating, or balancing diets may serve as temporary or healing regimens, but they are not necessarily appropriate as a long-term dietary lifestyle. For a mix of ethical, health, environmental, and esthetic reasons, I haven't eaten meat for about forty years, but this choice isn't for everyone. I tried a strict vegan diet (no animal products) for about five years, but I found that eating some dairy products (plus eggs) worked better for my needs. And in the past few years, I've started eating fish on rare occasions. I also ate no refined sugar products for a year but have since incorporated some sweets back into my diet.

Some of us seek perfect diets the way we might seek perfect soul mates, but let's not be intimidated by dietary true believers who presume to tell us the One True Way. Find out for yourself! Others may be experts on diet or medicine, but we're the experts on our own bodies. Listen to the counsel of the wise, but as in all things, experiment and see what works best for you.

Fasting

"This is your last meal for the next seven days." Soc proceeded to outline a purifying fast that I was to begin immediately. Diluted fruit juice and plain herb teas were to be my only fare....

"In a few years, there will be no need for rules. You can experiment and trust your instincts. For now, however, you're to avoid foods that contain refined sugar, refined flour, and meat, as well as coffee, alcohol, tobacco, or any other drugs. Focus on fresh fruits, vegetables, whole grains, and legumes. I don't believe in extremes, but for now, make breakfast a fresh fruit meal, with occasional yogurt. Your lunch, your main meal, should be a raw salad, baked or steamed potato, and whole-grain bread or cooked grains. Dinner should be a raw salad and, on occasion, lightly steamed vegetables.

Make good use of raw, unsalted seeds and nuts at every meal."

"I guess by now you're quite an expert on nuts, Soc," I grumbled.

Allowing Socrates to "put me on a program" may seem to contradict what I wrote earlier about not letting others tell us how to eat. However, Soc was recommending a temporary discipline to help me overcome my tendency toward being an unconscious omnivore. Just as a tennis coach might make technical recommendations, Socrates was making dietary recommendations.

Fasting can be a useful practice for many, but not for everyone. Most of us have an instinctive, childlike fear of not eating, which is natural, since growing children generally need regular nourishment and calories. (I don't recommend fasting for growing children, but there's no harm if they miss a meal once in a while or have no appetite when ill.)

As adults, periods of fasting (from food, the daily newspaper, the Internet, or television) can be wholesome disciplines with physical and psychological benefits. As with many things, fasting is best done in moderation. It's easy to get addicted to the feeling of purity and lightness. If you care to explore fasting for a few days or longer, it may be helpful to read a book on the subject or consult a health professional first. Except in medically supervised cases of treating obesity, fasting is *not* recommended for weight control. For maintaining an optimal weight, which differs from person to person, a moderate, long-lasting lifestyle of balanced diet and regular exercise remains the best approach.

Posture for Mind and Body

"Proper posture is a way of blending with gravity, Dan. Proper attitude is a way of blending with life."

Just as diet forms a foundation for how we live, so does posture. Posture is not just about sitting up straight but rather reflects our physical relationship to gravity in both stillness and motion. Posture affects digestion, breathing, and emotions. Yet this area of life is one of the least conscious for most of us, unless we start to suffer the chronic results of years of neglect and seek treatment.

Physical exercise is only as beneficial as the posture or form in which we do it. Many forms of bodywork, along with yoga, the Alexander technique, Feldenkrais, the Egoscue Method, and exercise systems such as Pilates, can help us to reintegrate and restore our natural ways of moving in the field of gravity.

Proper physical postures, referred to as *asanas* in yoga, are important to practice not just in classes but every moment of the day. Such conscious physical disciplines provide a strong foundation for practicing the peaceful warrior's way.

Walking a Different Path

While [my friends] ate their sundaes, I ordered mineral water and ended up sucking on a piece of ice. I looked at them enviously; they looked back at me as if I were a little crazy. And maybe they were right. Anyway, my social life was collapsing under the weight of my disciplines.

Whenever we improve or refine one of our habits or behaviors, we may find that friends, colleagues, loved ones, and peers take notice and offer comments or opinions. When one part of a system changes, it creates a pressure for another part to change, so it's natural for others to react to our changes.

More concretely, let's say Joe and Sally, a married couple, have both gotten out of shape from too much eating and too little exercise. Then let's say one of them decides to start a regular exercise routine and to eat less. Do you think the other spouse is going to cheer the first on and follow this good example? Perhaps, because a change in one person does create an innate pressure for the other to change as well. But the person "left behind" may sometimes engage in undermining behavior — expressing a wish, conscious or not, for the partner to go back to being the old Sally or Joe.

We humans constantly compare ourselves with, and even compete with, others. It isn't necessarily the most ideal or mature tendency, but it's a common one.

In the situation I described in the excerpt, when my friends were partying and enjoying desserts and I was following Soc's dietary disciplines, I felt isolated and had to take my friends' good-natured teasing when they noticed the change in my behavior — even though, by all accounts, it was a positive one.

People feel more comfortable around those who make them feel good about themselves, and our discipline may cause others to reflect on their own habits. So if we take a higher path, or just a different one, those who remain in place may feel less comfortable around us — our smoking or drinking buddies may even discourage our efforts to stop.

Walking a different path, no longer fitting in, can be a test of character. It may entail finding new friends who share our values. We have to deal with the fear that our changes in behavior or lifestyle may distance us from our spouses, partners, or friends. When moving into new and unfamiliar territory, explorers typically face the fear of separation, being cut off from the group. At times like these, we need to remember that we're not all here to fit in; some of us are here to lead.

If we're belittled by others who may feel threatened by a change we're making, we can ask ourselves, "Am I going to worship the god of opinion or listen to the god (or goddess) of my heart? Will I let others intimidate me into being more like them? Is fitting in such a high virtue? Or will I lead by example and give them the space to make their own choices as well?"

Maybe I was lucky. When I went through the changes I describe in *Way of the Peaceful Warrior*, my friends on the gymnastics team still accepted me due to our shared love of the sport — but I must have seemed strange to them at times. So it helped to have an understanding friend, teacher, and role model in Socrates.

When the Spiritual Honeymoon Is Over

Over time, though, I began to feel a growing resistance. I complained to Socrates, in spite of his dark look. "Soc, you're no fun anymore. You've become an ordinary grumpy old man; you never even glow."

He glowered at me. "No more magic tricks," was all he said. That was just it — no tricks, no sex, no potato chips, no hamburgers, no candy, no donuts, no fun, and no rest; only discipline inside and out.

You've probably heard the saying that everyone is an optimist in the first four hours of a diet. So when we make positive changes, take on new disciplines, or start new exercise routines or dietary regimens, we begin with enthusiasm and may even experience postive results in a relatively short time.

But inevitably, over time, we hit plateaus and find that with the peaks come valleys. Our disciplines are no longer new; they become routine (after three days or weeks or months or years). And at some point the initial passion or motivation wears thin. It's no longer fun telling friends about our new and exciting enterprise. All that's left is us and the daily decision to persist or not.

At this point in my training with Socrates, the newness had worn off and I had to confront my rising resistance and waning excitement. In this phase our old, familiar, and generally easier lifestyles call us back to the way things were. Fits of nostalgia fill our fantasy lives as doubts arise. After all, what was so bad about the way things were?

Applying willpower against the inertia of old habits is like applying friction to roll a boulder uphill; it creates psychic heat that has a purifying, empowering effect. But it burns just the same, and we hear the siren's sweet song, urging us to go back to the familiar, to be like everyone else, to be welcomed back into the fold, to take the pressure off.

Thus, to stop engaging in a destructive habit, such as smoking or binge drinking, it isn't enough to stop just once; we have to stop ourselves again and again, each and every time temptation arises — even when no one's praising us or cheering us on except ourselves. At times like this, remember these words attributed to Abraham Lincoln: "I desire so to live that if at the end, I have lost every other friend on earth, I shall at least have one friend left, and that friend shall be down inside of me."

From the transcendental view, whatever we do is perfect (no right or wrong, only consequences). We each have our own choices to make, our own lives to live. But at certain decision points, when we don't know which path to take, it may be helpful to ask, "What do I want to look back on ten years from now? What if my children faced this choice? What choice would I wish for them?"

Character is revealed through the choices we make under pressure. The choices we make and the actions we take after the honeymoon is over — when motivation fades and doubts arise

— are the true tests of character. If our behaviors are aligned with our highest aims, despite resistance or boredom or fear, then we continue to persist just one more hour, just one more day, along the peaceful warrior's way.

Overcoming Tendencies

I was through being a slave to random impulses.

That night marked the beginning of a new glow of self-respect and a feeling of personal power. I knew it would get easier now.

Small changes began to add up in my life. Ever since I was a kid, I'd suffered all kinds of minor symptoms, like a runny nose at night when the air cooled, headaches, stomach upsets, and mood swings, all of which I thought were normal and inevitable. Now they had all vanished.

I felt a constant sense of lightness and energy that radiated around me.

I did indeed feel better after making positive changes in my life. But my description in this excerpt — about feeling "a constant sense of lightness and energy" — was a bit idealized.

Nothing is constant; change is one of nature's operating principles. So it doesn't serve us to continually check for evidence of progress, moment to moment, to sustain our new behaviors. Even with the best of changes, we're still going to have ups and downs, moments of fatigue, even bouts of illness.

Promises of perfect health or constant energy do not match reality; still, our behaviors over time, along with our genetic constitutions, certainly influence our overall state of health and well-being. There's an old saying: "At fifty, we're responsible for our own face." Which is to say that the life we have lived will be reflected in our faces, and in our bodies. I wasn't thinking

about this as a young college athlete, but I had Socrates to remind me from the perspective of his years. The lifestyle I
adopted back then has served me well over time, as it can serve
anyone.

Even small changes can make noticeable differences over
time. We may not be able to completely overcome genetics
with lifestyle changes, but we do much good nonetheless. After
an arrow flies from the bow, the slightest course change in early
or midflight will have significant impact on its eventual direc-
tion. Just so, overcoming limiting or destructive tendencies and
habits pays dividends in both vitality and self-respect as the
seasons pass.

Progress and Pride

*I practiced breathing so slowly that it took one minute to complete
each breath. When combined with intense concentration and control
of specific muscle groups, this breathing exercise heated my body up
like a sauna and allowed me to remain comfortable outside no matter what the temperature.*

*I was excited to realize that I was developing the same power
that Socrates had shown me the night we met. For the first time, I
began to believe that maybe, just maybe, I could become a peaceful
warrior like him. Instead of feeling left out, I now felt superior to my
friends. When a friend complained of illness or other problems that
I knew could be remedied by simply eating properly, I offered what
advice I could.*

Training can lead to specific kinds of growth or progress. If we
do sit-ups over time, we get stronger; there's nothing especially
mysterious about the process. Regular practice demands and
develops spirit and discipline.

Concerning my description of being comfortable outside no matter what the temperature: Well, please forgive me for another slight exaggeration. Tibetan monks do indeed practice *tumo*, a sort of pressure-breathing method that increase body heat. Monks who engage in this practice are said to be able to sit in sub-freezing temperatures with naked bodies wrapped in wet sheets; the heat they generate not only keeps them warm but dries the sheets. While I did develop some capacity in this regard, continued practice is essential to maintaining this ability. And in practical terms, it takes less energy to wear warm clothing.

The central point of this excerpt was to show how I was beginning to feel superior to my friends because I had developed some unusual capacities. This kind of pride is as deluded as that of athletes (or of PhDs or poets) who think of themselves as superior by virtue of special training or abilities. No doubt, we can develop expertise or even some level of mastery in one or another area. But today, such physical abilities are less impressive to me than a demonstration of kindness and compassion.

Through practice, even as our minds become clearer and more focused, and our bodies more elastic, a sense of superiority (or inferiority) only reflects the illusion of separation, one of the hazards along the way. Humility comes from seeing our achievements (and struggles) in their proper perspective. Pride is beside the point. No one is better; no one is less. We are each and all simply being who we are, and doing what we do. No praise, no blame. Just living and learning.

Natural Breathing

"Don't worry, Dan. You just need to relax into life a little more. Now that you know what natural breathing feels like, you'll let yourself breathe naturally, more and more, until it starts to feel

normal. The breath is a bridge between mind and body, feeling and doing. Balanced, natural breathing brings you back to the present moment."

"Will it make me happy?"

"It will make you sane," he said.

In this selection, Joseph, the raw foods café owner and friend of Socrates, offered his own reminders for making me more conscious about the effects of food on my body and life, and about posture, tension, and breathing. He made sure that I paid special attention to the most precious, basic, and fundamental life skill: breathing.

It could be argued that we can go our entire lives without ever consciously working with the breath. It's an autonomic (automatic) and largely self-regulating system: When we need more air — for example, when we're exercising — we end up breathing more deeply. It's all quite natural.

In our daily lives, however, few of us breathe naturally. We might have done so as toddlers, when our little bellies expanded and relaxed with each breath. But as we grew through adolescence and into adulthood — sometimes long before — the mind imposed tension on the body, constricting the breath chronically, or at various times or in various circumstances.

Anyone who has taken on the discipline of paying attention to the breath for a single day, all day, will begin to notice (with some frustration, in my case) how many times we inhibit our breathing or cease it entirely — for example, when we concentrate on a fine-motor-control activity, sit on the toilet, experience emotional tension, hear an unexpected noise, or even pour some water or tea. The mind imparts tension, and tension inhibits breath.

Yogis and other devotees of physical culture have devised

esoteric breathing exercises for specific effects. Such disciplines are performed for a given period of time, similar to meditation.

And just as fasting helps free us from the fear of not eating, practices of holding our breath (fasting from air for brief periods) and practices of slow, deep breathing, sometimes to an extended count, can free us from the instinctive fear of not getting enough air. Gaining conscious control of the breath helps us, quite literally, to breathe easier.

As both Socrates and Joseph explained, the "ordinary disciplines" of the peaceful warrior's way pervade all of daily life. And one of the most healthful practices we can do is to attend to continuous breathing — relaxed and rhythmic, like the swing of a pendulum — throughout the day. We don't need to strain for deeper breaths but can simply practice simple, rhythmic breathing during all of our activities, letting the breath move the body. Such a practice may be simple, but it isn't easy. Nonetheless, it's another significant step on the path of personal evolution.

The Seduction of Spiritual Experience

"Don't get distracted by your experiences. Experiences come and go; if you want experiences, go to the movies; it's easier than all these yogas — and you get popcorn. Meditate all day, if you like; hear sounds and see lights, or see sounds and hear lights. But don't get seduced by experience. Let it all go!"

After my initial period of training with Socrates, during my travels I once sat before a charismatic spiritual teacher who taught a meditation technique that if practiced diligently might eventually reward me with a vision of the blue pearl (or maybe it was the blue camel). Those who reported seeing the blue pearl, or something like it, were granted high status as "mature practitioners."

But what do such visions, such peak experiences, mean to our daily lives? Do they help us to support our families, render service in the world, or show kindness to strangers? Seeking inner experiences as evidence of progress can become another search for achievement and status, only in a different arena.

Some more ethereal (and less grounded) people are prone to reporting "spiritual experiences" such as visions, blissful waves, *kriyas* (ecstatic trembling), and spontaneous movement, to the envy of others around them. Yet many spiritually mature individuals never experience such dramatic symptoms, altered states, or colorful visions.

Socrates took pains to emphasize that experiences, no matter how dramatic, all pass. It's not the experience that matters, but the lessons learned — measured by genuine, meaningful changes in our behaviors and perspectives.

Anger and Alchemy

After a moment of exquisite anger, I found myself laughing. He laughed, too, pointing at me. "Dan, you just experienced an alchemical transformation — you just transmuted anger to laughter."

Most of us can recall being upset — angry, sad, or even crying — and then having sudden shifts of perspective, only to find ourselves laughing. These moments of humor, of transcendence, aren't so different from the laughter generated by the punch line of a joke. In this upward shift to a larger perspective, what made us angry or sad now seems humorous, even silly or absurd. It's as if we suddenly remember that we're actors performing a scene in the drama of our lives. Seeing ourselves as characters on a stage, stepping out from behind our own eyes, we regain our sense of perspective.

That's the "alchemical transformation" to which Socrates was referring. The act of self-observation — the ability to make this shift from conventional seriousness to divine humor — is one of the most significant spiritual capacities we can develop. Restoring our sense of humor requires only the willingness and awareness to step outside ourselves, turn around, and see our dramas and antics and posturing from a distance.

Realism and Idealism

I heard his cry of anguish and saw him drop slowly to his knees and cry. By the time I reached him, his face was serene.

The fire chief came over to him and told him that the fire had probably started at the dry cleaner's next door. "Thank you," Joseph said.

"Joseph, I'm so sorry."

"Yes, me too," he replied with a smile.

"But a few moments ago you were so upset."

He smiled. "Yes, I was." I remembered Soc's words, "Let feelings flow, then let them go."

Some readers over the years have shared the puzzlement I described over Joseph's quick recovery from such a major loss. Here again, I admit to writing an idealized version of "emotional healing" in order to make a point. But it was never Soc's goal or my intention to present reality through rose-colored glasses.

When we explore spiritual and religious traditions, we encounter many idealistic notions, such as the idea that we can learn to think positive thoughts all or most of the time. When we read books about how to do this yet observe that it hasn't really worked in our personal experience, we may come to believe that if only we had truly applied ourselves, and done all the exercises, then we would have succeeded. And we may also believe that the authors of such books have positive thinking down to a fine art.

In reality, both positive and negative thoughts and feelings arise quite naturally: pleasant reveries, sad images, fears, doubts, and so forth. Thoughts are a problem only if we give them power or mistake them for reality.

Other idealistic notions include telling young men and women at the peak of the hormonal rush of puberty to abstain from sexual contact until marriage, or telling priests to remain celibate for life. With few exceptions, these idealistic recommendations don't work well for real people.

Now we return to the incident I described — finding Joseph in acute grieving for his café in flames, only to see him quickly relax, smile, and greet me as if nothing had happened. Joseph explained to me that he had developed an ability to "let it flow, and let it go." Good advice for anyone, which was why I wrote about this incident. But we can probably agree that the time frame was idealistic.

Real people generally need more time to "let it go." When someone asks me what to do about a broken heart, I can only answer, "You hurt." At least for a while. That's reality.

Ideals are absolutely essential; they represent what we strive for. Reality reflects who and where we are right now. Let's take both into account. Joseph or you or I have indeed suffered and survived loss and disappointment, experiencing grief and other emotions that heal, like wounds, over time. Some wounds leave scars and memories in their wake. This, too, is a natural part of our human experience, the peaceful warrior's way.

The Question of Habits

"Did I ever mention to you that there's no such thing as a bad habit?"...

"No, you didn't, and I've gone to great lengths to follow your recommendation to change my bad habits."

"That was to develop your will, you see, and to give your instincts a refresher course. You see, any unconscious, compulsive ritual is a problem. But specific activities — smoking, drinking, taking drugs, eating sweets, or asking silly questions — are both bad and good; every action has its price, and its pleasures. Recognizing both sides, you become realistic and responsible for your actions. Only then can you make the warrior's free and conscious choice — to do or not to do.

"There is a saying: 'When you sit, sit; when you stand, stand; whatever you do, don't wobble.' Once you make your choice, do it with all your spirit. Don't be like the preacher who thought about praying while making love to his wife, and thought about making love to his wife while praying....

"Whether or not my behavior meets your new standards, it should be clear to you that I have no compulsions or habits. My actions are conscious, spontaneous, intentional, and complete."

Socrates put out his cigarette, smiling at me. "You've become too stuffy, with all your pride and superior discipline. It's time we did a little celebrating."

Socrates would sometimes argue for one thing, then turn around and advocate its opposite, like the fabled Sufi sage Mullah Nasruddin, who approached a crowd of people gathered around two men, each arguing opposing views. "Calm down!" Nasruddin said. "What's the problem?" One of the combatants told his side of the story. "You're right!" Nasruddin snapped.

"But you haven't heard my side," yelled the other man.

Nasruddin heard him out, and responded with equal certainty, "You're right!"

"Wait a moment," said a bystander. "They can't *both* be right."

Scratching his head, Nasruddin replied, "You're right."

Everyone is right when seen from his or her own viewpoint, or from different angles.

There was once a spiritual teacher who would insist that undisciplined omnivores adopt a strict vegetarian diet, and who would take confirmed vegetarians fishing and insist they eat what they caught. Soc's words and behavior demonstrated that the good life is not founded upon a rigid set of rules or formulas but involves suppleness and strength as we move beyond our tendencies and so-called compulsions.

Soc first drew me into a disciplined, purifying diet and lifestyle, prescribing every sort of discipline so I would let go of my habitual self-indulgence. But when I had progressed to the point of puritan zeal, he said, "Watch out! If you get too self-righteous with all your disciplines, the *stress* is gonna kill you." So he took me out on the town to loosen me up.

Socrates based his teachings not on ideas of right and wrong but on the House Rule that actions have consequences — he took full responsibility for both the pleasures and the price of his choices. He pointed out that the addiction — the compulsive need to repeat any behavior — must be overcome. To him, an occasional cigarette or beer was not a problem. He might go weeks or months without smoking or drinking, then smoke a cigarette, then go a few more weeks or months before enjoying another smoke or drink.

But Soc was quick to point out that if someone is prone to physical addiction, whether from genetic predisposition or allergic craving — that is, if one drink always leads to another, as it does with some alcoholics — then it is best to avoid that activity altogether. There's no single rule for everyone.

It's all too easy to play the chronic puritan, or the habitual hedonist. Socrates could play either role as it suited him. Most of the time he lived in that balance place between self-indulgence and self-denial.

Moderation and the Passionate Life

"It's better to make a mistake with the full force of your being than to timidly avoid mistakes with a trembling spirit. Responsibility means recognizing both pleasure and price, action and consequence, then making a choice."

"It sounds so 'either-or.' What about moderation?"

"Moderation?" He leaped up on the desk. . . . "Moderation? It's mediocrity, fear, and confusion in disguise. It's the devil's dilemma. It's neither doing nor not doing. It's the wobbling compromise that makes no one happy. Moderation is for the bland, the apologetic, for the fence-sitters of the world afraid to take a stand. It's for those afraid to laugh or cry, for those afraid to live or die. Moderation" — he took a deep breath, getting ready for his final condemnation — *"is lukewarm tea, the devil's own brew!"*

"But you've told me the value of balance, the middle way, the golden mean."

Socrates scratched his head. "Well, you have a good point there."

Here we have another paradoxical section of the book, dealing with Soc's apparent disdain for moderation.

Throughout history, the sages of many cultures, from the Taoists Chuang Tzu and Lao Tzu to the Greek and Roman philosophers, have recommended the way of balance and moderation. In politics, centrists are usually given greater credibility than those at the extreme left or right (except by members of those extreme perspectives).

In everyday life, we accept that it's not good to eat or speak too fast or too slowly, or too loudly or too softly, for example. We wouldn't want to move too quickly or too slowly. The story of Goldilocks and the Three Bears contains this deep wisdom — one reason for its longevity as a popular children's tale.

Socrates lived a balanced life. His sense of relaxation and ease, the way he ate his food, the way he spoke, the way he moved — all reflected moderation. But he could also be passionate, and move rapidly when he wished, and explore extremes when it suited his instructive purposes.

Soc's little tirade about moderation was really addressed to those who are afraid to show passion, to speak up, to act dramatically, to stretch their limits or step outside their comfort zones. For such timid souls, "moderate" lives become mere comfort seeking, insulating them from any sense of excitement or adventure. These folks only take lukewarm showers, always go to sleep at the same reasonable time, and no longer remember staying up into the morning hours or getting into bed early with a good book or lover on occasion.

Socrates wasn't promoting a wild and crazy lifestyle — only making an impassioned argument for breaking routines — for being flexible, unreasonable, and full of life.

A Moment of Grace

Walking home, I was so overwhelmed with gratitude that I knelt outside my apartment and touched the earth. Taking a handful of dirt in my hand, I gazed up through emerald leaves shimmering in the breeze. For a few precious seconds, I seemed to slowly melt into the earth. Then, for the first time since I was a young boy, I felt a life-giving Presence without a name.

In these moments, I communed with a presence that was greater and more loving than anything I had ever known. It transcended all earthly problems and made everything okay, like a mother's embrace.

This experience seemed so obviously and eternally present, I later wondered why I wasn't aware of it all the time. An old proverb reminds us, "There's God; then there's not paying attention." Some people might use words like *reality* or *beauty* or *inspiration* instead of God. In any case, I hadn't been paying attention because I was caught up in the usual subliminal mutterings about my daily to-do lists and little problems.

A spiritual presence surrounds and embraces us, right now and in every moment. We're not likely to hear the weather forecaster announce, "There's a twenty percent chance of rain, and thirty percent chance of spirit out today."

The truth is, there's no lack of divine support and nourishment; we're never abandoned. We have only to find the free attention to look above and beyond. At their best, that's what religion and spiritual practices are all about. The practices and rituals, the chanting, singing, and prayers, are simply ways to draw our attention to the eternal presence I felt on that quiet evening, in a moment of grace.

When Death Calls

"Socrates, aren't you upset, just a little?"

He laid the wrench down. "That reminds me of a story I heard a long time ago, about a mother who was overcome with grief by the death of her young son.

"'I can't bear the pain and sorrow,' she told her sister.

"'My sister, did you mourn your son before he was born?'

"'No, of course not,' the despondent woman replied.

"'Well, then, you need not mourn for him now. He has only returned to the same place, his original home, before he was ever born.'"

"Is that story a comfort to you, Socrates?"

"Well, I think it's a good story. Perhaps in time you'll appreciate it," he replied brightly.

"I thought I knew you well, Socrates, but I never knew you
could be so heartless."

"No cause for worry, Dan — death is perfectly safe."

"But he's gone!"

Soc laughed softly. "Maybe he's gone, maybe not. Maybe he
was never here!" His laughter rang through the garage.

I suddenly realized why I was so troubled. "Would you feel the
same way if I had died?"

"Of course!" He laughed. "Dan, there are things you don't yet
understand. For now, just think of death as a transformation — a
bit more radical than puberty, but nothing to get particularly upset
about. It's just one of the body's changes. When it happens, it happens. The warrior neither seeks death nor flees from it."

His face grew more somber before he spoke again. "Death is not
sad; the sad thing is that most people don't really live at all." That's
when his eyes filled with tears.

Like mystics and monks and sages, and those who have "died"
and been brought back, Socrates no longer feared the inevitable
event that most of us would rather not think about.

Every beginning requires an ending. Or perhaps not really
an ending, but another revolution around the wheel of life.
Leaves come loose in autumn, to be replaced by new buds in
spring. It's the way of nature, the way of the universe. Those
fallen leaves become compost to nourish the earth and new
growth. From the point of view of the leaf, it's death; from the
point of view of the tree and soil, it's a welcome thing.

We are each given a lifetime, or maybe many lifetimes, but

since we typically don't remember them, it may be best to live this life as if it's the only one we have. Most of us are cold and disoriented at birth, are afraid or uncomfortable at death, and have an even worse time at puberty! But what major transition is easy?

Soc reminded me that we die and are born each day, passing through the void, then awakening in the morning. Each day we create effects, leave traces of unfinished business that we may have to resolve in the days to follow. Perhaps it's the same with lifetimes.

From a conventional view, death is real, and often tragic — we lose all our friends and loved ones, through either their death or ours. Loss and grieving are natural parts of life. No one who has sat with a dying parent or friend and seen the body afterward — the empty shell — can deny the reality of death.

Socrates spoke of death from a transcendent view of who we truly are — the awareness shining behind and through billions of eyes. From this point of view, death is merely a drop of water merging with the great sea — hardly an earthshaking event.

Even now, millions of living creatures are dying and being born on this planet, some of them human beings. Creatures are devouring other creatures, all in a dynamic play of change, all perfectly natural.

There are some who propose that life is an opportunity to prepare well for a good death — clarifying our awareness to make a conscious transition to what follows. And I look forward to my own death, when I'll discover for myself what, if anything, comes next. But in the meantime I'm going to live as long and as fully as I can, for each day is another day to learn, to teach, to serve.

The main thing is to die after having truly lived, after leaving behind a contribution. Socrates lived fully and was perfectly content to let go when the time came. As the Native American saying goes, "Today is a good day to die."

It's also a good day to live.

ON CHAPTER FIVE
THE MOUNTAIN PATH

A knowledge of the path
cannot be substituted for
putting one foot in front of the other.

— M. C. RICHARDS

Answers from Within

"You're going to have to find the answers from within. Beginning now — go out back, behind the station, behind the trash bin. There, in the corner of the lot, against the wall, you'll find a large flat stone. Sit on that stone until you have something of value to tell me."

In asking me to find my answers from within, Socrates set out to balance my psyche and my life. Prior to meeting him, I was, like most Westerners, indoctrinated in an externalized, techno-logical, information-devouring, outward-seeking consumer society. Soc challenged me to trust my "inner knower" and find something of value inside. He wouldn't tolerate my parroting something I had read or been told; as a college student, I was already good at that.

Soc called me to respect and draw upon that infinite intelligence to which we all have access, if we only look, listen, and trust. Few of us fully trust our innate connection to what Carl Jung called the *collective unconscious*. Soc was waiting for me to discover this vast repository of cell-level wisdom within.

Practically speaking, if we want to learn to play golf or explore any new skill, we may benefit from training with an experienced guide, coach, or teacher. But we're wise not to let external guidance overshadow our inner knowers, our moral compass — the spark of divine intelligence that is our human treasure.

Socrates insisted that I answer my own questions to wean me of relying on him. He encouraged me to turn to the source of guidance within each human heart, where the higher self speaks.

Something Worth Sharing

I wondered, still standing on the rock, why that incident came to me. Then it hit me; I walked into the office, stood before Soc's desk, and announced, "There are no ordinary moments!"

Readers of *Way of the Peaceful Warrior* may recall that I sat out on that rock — or on a car in the movie version — until I had "something worthwhile" to share. It took many hours of exhaustive contemplation, and many false starts, before I could find a genuine insight — the realization that "there are no ordinary moments."

The danger in simply reading this phrase is that it, too, can become a bromide, an affirmation, a cliché. "Yes, of course," we might think. "A good reminder. Heard it before." But when this realization penetrates us to our core, our life changes — we begin to give the world our undivided attention.

We do not remember days; we remember moments. Life is a series of moments. And no matter what our opinions or beliefs, it remains a universal truth that the quality of each moment determines the quality of our lives.

Socrates reminded me that athletes practice athletics, poets practice poetry, musicians practice music — but *peaceful warriors practice everything*. Most of us have stopped practicing; we only go through the motions — brushing our teeth, cooking dinner, and doing all sorts of things we have done hundreds of times before with no real attention. Practice involves doing with the conscious intention to improve, to refine, so that each day, each moment, we commit to walking more smoothly, breathing more fully, and practicing everything we used to merely do. Practicing draws us into the present moment and makes every moment extraordinary.

At random times during the day, ask yourself: "Am I merely doing, or am I practicing what I'm doing?"

A Matter of Perspective

"You must go far beyond normal, beyond the usual, common, or reasonable, to reach the realm of the warrior. You've always tried to become superior in an ordinary realm. Now you're going to become ordinary in a superior realm."

Again, is there a "realm of the warrior" waiting for us? Yes, absolutely — but only speaking metaphorically. We find the warrior's realm in this world, in this moment; we don't have to travel out of our bodies or to other dimensions to discover the peaceful warrior's way. Wherever we step, the path appears beneath our feet.

As Socrates emphasized, and I echo once again, we're all peaceful warriors in training — even now, as we struggle with our human condition, evolving through daily life with its gauntlet of challenges in relationships, health, work, and finances.

As a star college athlete, I had been a big fish in a little sea, but I was soon humbled as I entered a new frame of reference, an expansive arena with higher standards and greater demands, where I had to let go of my quest for superiority and accept my humanity.

When I was young I felt small and less capable around the older, bigger kids, but strong and wise when playing with friends younger than I. I came to understand, even then, that there would always be those with greater or lesser abilities, and there was little point in comparing myself with others.

Since we're ultimately all one body and one spirit, any sense of superiority or inferiority is illusion. Should the arm compare itself with the leg? Should the brain feel superior to the heart?

There is no superior, no inferior — only all of us here, together, growing and evolving. This is the perspective that Socrates would want me to convey.

The Bone Massage

"You move well, Dan, compared to most people, but your muscles hold too much tension. Tense muscles require more energy to move. So you have to learn how to release stored tension. . . .

"By now you can appreciate how the mind imposes tension on the body. Worries, anxieties, and other mental debris are stored as chronic tension. Now it's time for you to release these tensions and free your body from the past....

"Now, do exactly as I do." He began by rubbing a sweet-scented oil over his left foot. I copied every step as he squeezed, pressed, and dug very deeply into the bottom, top, sides, and between the toes, stretching, pressing, and pulling. "Massage the bones, not just the flesh and muscle — deeper," he said. Half an hour later, we were through with the left foot. We repeated the process with the right foot. This went on for hours, covering every part of the body. I learned things about my muscles, ligaments, and tendons I'd never known before. I could feel where they were attached; I could feel the shape of the bones.

Over time, our worries, anxieties, attachments, resistance, and fear impose chronic tension on our bodies. So our current state of tension or ease reflects cumulative incidents from the past. We store the past not just in our memories, but in the muscles and connective tissue of our bodies. Many systems aim to clear old traumas and emotional charge from our psyches, but more work is necessary to clear the past from our bodies.

We can treat our psyches like archeological digs, shoveling up layers of debris. As fascinating as such work may be, beneath one layer we only find another. By working directly on a physical level — clearing chronic and accumulated tension — we rejuvenate our bodies, returning to a more childlike state and allowing for more efficient movement, greater energy, and faster healing. Rather than seeking happiness in our minds, we can, in a practical way, create happier, more peaceful bodies.

Self-massage — such as the bone massage Socrates taught

me — is one approach to clearing away debris from the past. By taking responsibility for working on myself, I came to truly know myself to the bone. But this is only one way to come to know the body and clear the inevitable tensions and imbalances that can accumulate over time. We can also explore healthful forms of conscious exercise such as yoga, tai chi, or chi gung as direct physical means to liberate our bodies from the past, enjoy the present, and enrich the future as we travel along the peaceful warrior's way.

Satori and the Way

"Now let me tell you about satori, *a Zen concept. Satori occurs when attention rests in the present moment, when the body is alert, sensitive, relaxed, and the emotions are open and free. Satori is the warrior's state of being."*

"You know, Soc, I've had that feeling many times, especially during competitions. Often I'm concentrating so hard, I don't even hear the applause."

"Yes...challenging activity can serve as a gateway to satori... draws you into the moment of truth...."

"This is why gymnastics is one of the warrior's arts, a way to focus the mind and free the emotions as you train the body. But most athletes fail to expand this clarity into daily life. This is your task. And when satori becomes your everyday reality, we will be equals. Satori is your key to the gate."

Satori, a word that has no precise equivalent in the English language, refers to those moments when body, mind, and emotion are so integrated and aligned that they form a whole, greater than the sum of its parts. We sometimes call that whole by the name *spirit* — as in "That's the spirit!"

Performance artists, world-class athletes, warriors, and monks practicing moving meditation experience moments of satori (referred to in the West as *the zone*). We've all experienced satori, or the zone, in those moments when head, heart, and physical vitality worked in harmony. At such times, amazing things can happen in sports and other pursuits.

Socrates was less concerned with my winning medals than with my living more and more in this aligned state in everyday life, when the doer disappears and all that remains is movement and flow. The paradox, as Soc once pointed out to me, is that when "I" have achieved this state of immersion, I have found the key to the gateway — but there's no one left to walk through.

The Art of Nonresistance

"The true martial arts teach nonresistance — the way of the trees bending in the wind. This attitude is far more important than physical technique."

Using the principles of aikido, Socrates was able to throw me without any apparent effort, no matter how I tried to push him, grab him, punch him, or even tackle him. "Never struggle with anyone or anything. When you're pushed, pull; when you're pulled, push. Find the natural course and bend with it. Join with nature's power." His actions proved his words. . . .

In the gym I did my best to apply what I'd learned, "letting movements happen" instead of trying to do them.

An easeful, flowing attitude reflects the spiritual law of surrender, acceptance, nonresistance — no longer struggling, but going with, using, and harnessing what arises and guiding that force, that energy, that circumstance with grace. True in martial arts, true in daily life.

This kind of flow takes practice; our usual habit is to resist, resent, expect, hold on, or rigidify. Like stubborn children whose arms have to be pulled by their parents, we put on the brakes and pull the other way. It takes time, clear intention, and practice to form the habit of first *going with*. If we had to swim across a powerful river, it wouldn't be wise to try to swim against the current (as we often do in everyday life); we'd be better off letting the waters carry us as we gently angled toward the far shore.

The martial arts of aikido, tai chi, and Soc's native Russian art, now called *systema*, utilize this relaxed, natural practice of nonresistance — enabling students to explore a new way of moving and being. But the peaceful warrior's way truly comes to fruition not only on the sports field or martial arts *dojo* but, as always, in the midst of everyday life.

Meditation in Action

"Meditating an action is different from doing it. To do, there is a doer, a self-conscious 'someone' performing. But when you meditate an action, you've already released attachment to outcomes. There's no 'you' left to do it. In forgetting yourself, you become what you do, so your action is free, spontaneous, without ambition, inhibition, or fear."

In Professor Eugen Herrigel's classic book *Zen in the Art of Archery*, he describes his first day at a Japanese school of Zen archery — *kyudo*, the "way of the bow" — when he was asked to shoot an arrow into the straw target around ten meters away. He had practiced some archery back in Germany, where he taught Asian studies, so he eagerly notched the arrow, aimed, and watched as the arrow pierced the bull's-eye. He turned with some pride to see the archery master shaking his head in displeasure.

This made no sense at all to Herrigel and his external, goal-oriented training. It was only after many months of study that he came to understand that the goal of *kyudo* was not merely external show but the internal state of satori, the egoless shot, when there was no separate achiever doing the shooting — only bow, arrow, pulling, arrow flying. To put this in more Western terms, the body does the shooting without any sense of an "I" being in control.

One day nearly a year after he began, Herrigel stood and breathed softly, and the arrow notched and flew — and hit the corner of the straw bale. The master yelled, "*Hai!* Yes!" And Herrigel realized what had happened — a selfless, natural action, without fear, attachment, or ambition. There was no one to succeed, no one to fail; no credit, no blame.

Later Herrigel had an opportunity to ask, "Sensei, I finally understand the internal purpose of my training — but is it not also important to be able to shoot with accuracy?"

The master took the bow and stood facing the target. "Turn off the lights!" he instructed. Herrigel did so. In the darkness, he heard a *thwak!* as an arrow struck the target, then a second *thwak*. "Lights on," said the master.

When Herrigel's eyes adjusted, he saw two arrows in the center of the bull's-eye — one had nearly split the other in the darkness. He found out later that his Zen archery master had established a record of twelve hundred bull's-eyes in a row. Meditation in action.

When the ego isn't running the show, the show still goes on — even more effectively, as it turns out.

What might the quality of our lives become if we meditated

all our daily actions of eating, walking, speaking — letting them all happen naturally, spontaneously, without a tense doer holding tightly to the controls? This egoless action is what the Zen masters mean when they advise you to "die even while you live."

It took me considerable time to embody this core teaching of Socrates — to loosen my tight grip, to get out of my own way, and to die in each moment so that I might truly live.

Reality's Reminders

"The House Rules reveal that you can control your efforts, not outcomes. Do your best; let God handle the rest."

A primary cause of daily anxiety and frustration in the face of life's inevitable changes and inconveniences is our lack of understanding about what we can and cannot control.

We can control our behavior, and that's pretty much it. Unless we have a related disability, we can will ourselves to say a kind word, tie a shoelace, and control numerous other behaviors.

We may apply all sorts of techniques and strategies to shift our emotions and thoughts (which may work on occasion), but we can't consistently will ourselves to stop negative thoughts or troubling emotions. However, thoughts and feelings all pass, so we can treat them like bees buzzing in nearby flowers and let them be.

We're not responsible for the thoughts or emotions that arise and pass, out of our control, but we *are* responsible for what we do. And that holds true no matter what our childhoods were like or what moods we find ourselves in.

We can control our efforts, but not the outcomes. No matter how hard we work, we cannot guarantee that we'll sink that putt, find love, or succeed in business. However, by making the effort, we increase the likelihood of achieving our goals. And as basketball great Michael Jordan once said, "You make zero percent of the shots you don't take." Since effort is all we can control, our efforts themselves represent moments of success on the peaceful warrior's path.

PLEASURE BEYOND THE MIND

There is surely nothing other
than the single purpose of the present moment.
A person's life is a succession of moment after moment.
When one fully understands this moment,
there will be nothing else to do
and nothing else to pursue.

— YAMAMOTO TSUNETOMO

A Childhood Revisited

"You once were bathed in brightness, and found pleasure in the simplest things." With that, he took my head in his hands and sent me back to my infancy.

My eyes open wide. They gaze intently at shapes and colors beneath my hands as I crawl on the tiled floor. I touch a rug and it touches me back. Everything is bright and alive....

Some time later. Cool air touches my face as I crawl in a garden. Colorful flowers tower around me, and I'm surrounded by new smells. I tear one and bite it; my mouth is filled with a bitter message. I spit it out.

My mother comes. I hold out my hand to show her a wiggly black thing that tickles my hand. She reaches down and knocks it away. "Nasty spider!" she says. Then she holds a soft thing to my face; it talks to my nose. "Rose," she says, then makes the same noise again. "Rose." I look up at her, then around me, and drift again into the world of scented colors.

I came to lying facedown on Soc's yellow rug. I lifted my head to peer at the legs of his ancient oak desk. But now everything seemed somehow dimmed. "Socrates, I feel half asleep, like I need to douse myself with cold water and wake up. Are you sure that last journey didn't do some damage?"

"No, Dan, the damage was done over the years, in ways you'll soon see."

"That place... it was like the Garden of Eden."...

"Every infant lives in a bright Garden where everything is sensed directly, without the veils of thought — free of beliefs, interpretation, and judgments.

"You 'fell' from grace when you began thinking, about — when you became a namer and a knower....

"You've learned names and categories for everything: 'That's good, that's bad, that's a table, that's a chair, that's a car, a house, a flower, dog, cat, chicken, man, woman, sunset, ocean, star.'"

Until I met Socrates, I never really understood the words attributed to Jesus of Nazareth about the need to become "like little children to enter the kingdom of heaven." Most of us now grasp that "the kingdom of heaven" is within, and that the biblical quotation refers to a child's relative clarity of perception, prior to the encrustation of our complex adult filters. In this way, a young child has certain qualities akin to a Zen master's, but with a significant difference: In an infant, the ego is undeveloped; in a Zen master, the ego is transcended.

My revisit to the garden of clear, bright, undiluted perception — and later my fall from grace into the labels, meanings, and beliefs that obscure direct perception — was intended to create for my readers an understanding of what has happened to us all.

Consider how infants gaze, wide-eyed, into mystery. They don't know what anything is. No meanings, opinions, interpretations, expectations, or judgments. Infants experience everything just as it is, until it becomes interpreted for them by a parent ("Nasty spider!"). Some interpretations — such as teaching children not to run across the street without looking — are necessary parts of our socialization and survival.

Be that as it may, by the time we're ten years old, we no longer see the world as it is. So a part of our training (or, more accurately, deprogramming) involves an objective observation of the perceptual filters that separate us from our environment. Once we detect the distortions and "dirt" on our windows to the world, we can "clean" them to reawaken the state of clear, fresh perception, innocence, and openness, which I described in that visionary return to my childhood.

A Warrior's Way to Wealth

His response, as usual, shocked me. "As a matter of fact, Dan, I'm quite wealthy. One must become rich to be happy." He smiled at my dumbfounded expression, picked up a pen from his desk, and wrote on a clean white sheet of paper:

Happiness = Satisfaction/Desires

"You are rich if you have enough money to satisfy all your desires. So there are two ways to be rich: You earn, inherit, borrow, beg, or steal enough money to meet all your desires; or, you cultivate a simple lifestyle of few desires; that way you always have enough money.

"A peaceful warrior has the insight and discipline to choose the simple way — to know the difference between needs and wants. We have few basic needs but endless wants. Full attention to every moment is my pleasure. Attention costs no money; your only investment is training.... The secret of happiness, you see, is not found in seeking more, but in developing the capacity to enjoy less."

There's a significant difference between wants and needs. This insight is not in itself so radical, but its application is profound, given the ego's deep conditioning to acquire, possess, amass. Shopping for "something new" is both a diversion and a passion for many. How exciting to purchase a new house, car, gadget, shoes, or other apparel. There's nothing wrong with commerce — countless people buy and sell in a flowing economy. The problem is when shopping becomes an addiction, and we confuse wants with needs.

We need basic shelter, food, and water. If we have nourishing food, water, and shelter (and a healthful environment), then we have what we need. All the rest are extras. Those of us who are fortunate enough to live in a developed nation, and who have also created some level of abundance beyond simple sustenance, can enjoy a cornucopia of extras. Bless such folks! Bless us all! Let's not begrudge others their rest and recreation, their comfortable cars or even swimming pools. Enjoy! But neither should we confuse extras with essentials.

Some of us are content with relatively simple lives, while others have millions of dollars and may still crave more experience, more things. Some of us have few possessions but abound in the riches of loving friends and family. By cultivating simplicity, seeing through the empty promises of accumulated possessions, we can, as the Sufis say, be "in the world but not of the world."

How we view the world is a function of where we stand. As appealing as the idea of living simply might be to some of us, our needs and wants may change depending upon where we live and whether we're married or have children (for whom we want a high-quality education). Then there's a house with a mortgage, and gas and electricity and doctor's bills, and insurance and the other aspects of life in the real world.

An extremely simple, need-based lifestyle worked fine for me when I was young and could live on little. Later, Joy and I rented some tiny apartments, but over time, as our family grew, our lifestyles changed. We once sat on an old couch acquired from Goodwill and read books borrowed from the library or watched a small television sitting atop an apple crate. Eventually the television got bigger and was moved to our home gym. Our daughters are now college graduates. Someday Joy and I may once again downsize and simplify — all part of the coming and going, the rhythms of life in society, the changing flux of wants and needs.

Possessions and changing fortunes don't mean much in terms of happiness, but they are the stuff of life, and one aspect of the peaceful warrior's way.

I conclude this commentary on material wealth with the story of a young journalist who traveled to Poland to interview a respected rabbi. When he entered the rabbi's living quarters, a simple room furnished only with a cot, a single shelf with books, and a small desk, the reporter was moved to ask, "Rabbi, where is your furniture?"

"Well, where is *your* furniture?" the rabbi responded.

"My furniture?" asked the puzzled journalist. "But — I'm just passing through..."

"So am I," said the rabbi. "So am I."

Back to the Present

"The only thing you know absolutely is that you are here, wherever here may be. From now on, whenever your attention begins to drift off to other times and places, I want you to snap back. Remember, the time is now and the place is here....

"You can do nothing to change the past, and the future will never come exactly as you expect or hope for. There have never been past warriors, nor will there be future ones. The warrior is here, now. Your sorrow, your fear and anger, regret and guilt, your envy and plans and cravings live only in the past, or in the future."

"Hold on, Socrates. I distinctly remember being angry in the present."

"Not so," he said. "What you mean is that you acted angry in a present moment. Action always happens in the present, because it is an expression of the body, which can only exist in the here and now. But the mind is like a phantom that lives only in the past or future. Its only power over you is to draw your attention out of the present....

"Just keep your attention in the present moment, Dan. This is freedom from suffering, from fear."

If there's a primary teaching, a repeated theme, in *Way of the Peaceful Warrior*, it comes down to the present moment, the moment of reality. This reminds me of the time a high school student told me that he couldn't attend a workshop but asked me if I could give him a few words of good advice. I answered, *"Here and now, breathe and relax."* If this young man applied and practiced the principles behind these six words — if he made them a central focus in his life — there would not be much more he would have to learn.

In this moment, we have only one thing to do, only one place to be.

We can of course recall memories of the past, or plan the day to come. But it's best not to get too attached to our plans, because they have a way of changing. In fact, as that familiar saying goes, "If you want to make God laugh, tell God your plans."

Most of our dissatisfaction and disappointment stem from thoughts about past or future. The past or the future may overwhelm us (for example, when we wake up before dawn and think of traumas from years gone by, or the many things we have to do later that day), but we can always handle what's in front of us right now. We can control only what we do in this present moment, and the quality of our moments becomes the quality of our lives.

Our lives involve many duties. Yet life becomes profoundly simple when we remember that *we can only do one thing at a time*. Attend to this, and all will be well.

Career Advice in Brief

I'd finished my university education.

I brought fresh apple juice to the station to celebrate with Socrates. As we sat and sipped, my thoughts again drifted into the future.

"Where are you?" Soc asked. "What time is it?"

"Here. Now. But my present reality is that I need a career. Any advice?"

"Yes. Do what you will. Follow your nose and trust your instincts."

"That's not entirely helpful."

"It doesn't matter what you do, only how well you do it."

Soc's closing line of career advice puzzled me for a long time. It seemed like saying, "It doesn't matter who you marry, as long as you make a go of it." But given that we each have personal values, talents, and interests, it probably *does* matter, at least in a conventional sense, what career or partner we choose. In fact, our choices of work and partner may be among the most important we'll ever make. Both are worth considerable soul searching.

However, I think Socrates wanted to emphasize that the most important thing isn't to keep searching obsessively for the perfect job or mate, but to choose and then to approach the work (or relationship) with the utmost quality.

From a cosmic view (Soc's usual perspective), few things are as serious as we may believe. So whatever we choose is grist for the mill, all part of our peaceful warrior training in the *dojo* of daily life.

Still, most of us benefit from a period of self-examination and experimentation (especially in our teens and twenties), so that we can prepare for and pursue a career that best suits our interests and talents — work that we find meaningful and ful-filling.

Such fulfillment wasn't always part of the equation. My father came of age during the Great Depression, when men traveled far from home to find any kind of work they could to support their families. The work didn't have to be meaningful; it just needed to pay. Today, the quest for meaningful work seems worthwhile, because the process requires self-examination and self-knowledge and calls us to face our doubts and consider what we're willing to do to reach our goals.

But it still comes down to attention to quality, to doing the work well. Years ago, while waiting for a train to Kyoto, I watched a small, middle-aged man as he carefully polished one of hundreds of shining metal posts supporting a railing that ex-tended far down the platform. He must have spent nearly a full

minute on each post. It seemed to me that I had discovered a
Zen master, someone who understood that what matters is not
so much what we do, but how well we do it. Therein lies the satisfaction we seek.

Socrates found meaning and satisfaction in being the best
service station mechanic he could be. Ever since my time with
him, whatever form of work or service I performed, I've done
my best to follow his example.

ON BOOK THREE

UNREASONABLE HAPPINESS

*The older you get, the more you realize
that kindness is synonymous
with happiness.*

—— LIONEL BARRYMORE

ON CHAPTER SEVEN

THE FINAL SEARCH

We travel the world over
in search of what we need
and return home to find it.

— GEORGE MOORE

Weak Link, Strong Spirit

"No matter how strong we appear, each of us has a hidden weakness that may be our ultimate undoing. House Rules: For every strength there is a weakness — and for every weakness, a strength."

We all have strengths and weaknesses, flaws and virtues. Socrates explained that his heart was one of his weak links. It was difficult for me to accept this reality. (How easily we project power and perfection onto those we admire, placing them on lofty pedestals, and how quick we are to pull them down when we discover a single flaw!)

Even the most renowned spiritual masters have human bodies, urges, quirks, foibles, and frailties. We all have sages and fools within us, waiting to take turns onstage. In my experience, individuals with the greatest gifts or powers often have weaknesses of similar scope. And those of us with disabilities or challenges often develop compensating strengths and other admirable qualities.

Our greatest strengths and most profound frailties may remain hidden for a time — until a dire adversity or a great demand calls them forth. Socrates brought out both my liabilities and my deepest resources. A teacher or guide may serve this function but isn't always necessary, since our daily lives will eventually call forth all the courage and love that we have within us as we travel up the mountain path.

Courage and Love

"You haven't yet opened your heart fully, to life, to each moment. The peaceful warrior's way is not about invulnerability, but absolute vulnerability — to the world, to life.... A warrior's life is not about imagined perfection or victory; it is about love...."

"Socrates, tell me about love. I want so much to understand."

"Love is not something to be understood; it can only be lived."

We usually envision a warrior with armor and shield, protected from the slings and arrows of the world. But for those of us who strive for peaceful hearts and warrior spirits, life is not about hiding behind armor, poised to defend ourselves at the least provocation. Rather, the peaceful warrior's way is a call to open up, to become as transparent and as vulnerable as young children. This may be one of the greatest powers of all. As the founder of aikido, Morehei Uyeshiba, once said, "Aikido is invincible because it contends with nothing."

The Taoists point out how the flexible overcomes the rigid. The wise bend with force like young saplings and embrace criticism before speaking their truth: "Yes, you have a good point — and here's another way of looking at it." There are few things we cannot accomplish by remaining soft, open, transparent, and vulnerable — yielding one moment, while being assertive another.

Then we come to Soc's words about love, reminding us that love cannot be understood, only lived. I had tried to understand love, but it was like trying to derive the square root of a sonnet. Even today, love remains a mystery. It has taken me years to realize that a warrior's love is not merely a feeling, but an action. I cannot control whether I feel loving (or grateful or kind) in any given moment, but I can behave with lovingkindness.

Thus, bringing love into the world is not about waiting for the right mood or emotion to emerge but rather entails deliberate, expansive acts of generosity we can call forth at will.

Live with Passion, Teach by Example

"Better to live until you die," he said. "I am a warrior, so my way is action. I am a teacher, so I teach by example. Some day you may teach others as I have taught you — then you'll understand that words are not enough; you, too, must teach by example what you've realized through experience."

When Socrates said, "Better to live until you die," it seemed like transparent advice, since we have no choice but to do just that.

But Soc wasn't talking about merely existing until we expire; he meant living fully, with attention and feeling, as if each moment — each touch of a loved one or taste of food or view of a sunset — were our last.

Then Soc shifted to the topic of teaching by example: We all teach who we are, not just what we say. Socrates, like his ancient Greek counterpart, used words with care and respect, but his most powerful influence on me came from how he lived — how he moved, spoke, and behaved — with courage and compassion.

His example served as a model I could aspire to, and showed that it was possible to live in accord with a higher path than the one I had previously followed.

I now appreciate that all the words I've written in my books — and all those I've spoken in my lectures and seminars and workshops — count less than how I behave day to day in my relationships with others. This is equally true for all of us as we travel together on the winding path of personal growth.

The Greatest Powers

"I was hoping you would bypass any fascination with powers... what do you want to know?"

"Well, for starters, foretelling the future. You seem to be able to do it sometimes."

"Reading the future is based on a realistic perception of the present. Don't be concerned about seeing the future until you can clearly see the present....

"Special powers do in fact exist, Dan. But for the warrior, such things are beside the point. Don't be deluded by shiny baubles. A warrior can rely on the power of love, of kindness, of service — and

the power of happiness. You cannot attain happiness; it attains you — but only after you surrender everything else."

Some of us inclined toward magical thinking are fascinated by ideas of special powers (like levitation, extrasensory perception, or out-of-body travel) that might distinguish us or set us apart from other mere mortals. Such abilities, we're told, come from austere practices and purification, or secret teachings and special techniques — and if we concentrate and meditate enough, do special breathing, or stretch into yogic shapes, we may gain these special powers. Even if we could develop special powers, would they make us happy for long?

Extraordinary abilities, I must admit, do have a certain appeal. When I was young and first saw the play *Peter Pan*, there was nothing in the world I wanted more than to fly, to levitate, to soar! If only I could have found some of that pixie dust, if only I could have generated enough happy thoughts — but I had to settle for becoming a trampoline champion and discover that on earth whatever goes up must come down.

Without doubt, we can refine our instincts and sharpen our intuitive abilities; we can develop more vital energy through healthful practices and enjoy more youthful, pliable, and relaxed bodies. We can certainly experience more moments of perspective, mental clarity, and peace as we commune with that divine spirit that interpenetrates our world. So there are real benefits from "doing the work." Not because we have discovered new dimensions, but because we have developed different eyes.

Setting aside the issue of special powers, Socrates turned back to the topic of happiness, referring to it as the watched pot that never boils. As Thoreau wrote, "Happiness is like a butterfly:

The more you chase it, the more it eludes you. But if you turn your attention to other things, it comes and sits softly on your shoulder."

Soc's approach to happiness might best be expressed by George Bernard Shaw: "Never mind likes and dislikes; they are of no consequence. Just do what must be done. This may not be happiness, but it is greatness."

This statement, as well as any other, reflects the heart of the peaceful warrior's way.

The Way Creates the Warrior

"A warrior is not something you become, Dan. It is something you either are, in this moment, or something you are not. The Way itself creates the warrior."

Uruguayan novelist Juan Carlos Onetti said, "I am not a writer except when I write." The same holds for anything we do. A doctor out on the golf course is a golfer, not a doctor (unless someone suddenly needs a physician). We are what we're doing in the moment.

So we cannot strive to become peaceful warriors in the future. There's no degree to be earned. We either behave like warriors in the present moment, or we don't. Some moments my actions reflect a warrior spirit, and other times they don't. If anything sets any of us apart, it's that we live a higher proportion of such moments.

Life develops what it demands; the way creates the warrior. Daily life is a form of spiritual weight lifting to strengthen our spirits. So when the road gets bumpy, let's roll up our sleeves and remember that the difficulties we face are our training, and we can make the choice to face them squarely, as peaceful warriors in training.

Happiness Now

"Consider your fleeting years, Danny. One day you'll discover that death is not what you might imagine; but then, neither is life. Either may be wondrous, filled with change; or, if you do not awaken, both may turn out to be a considerable disappointment....

"Wake up! If you knew for certain that you had a terminal illness — if you had little time left to live — you would waste precious little of it! Well, I'm telling you, Dan — you do have a terminal illness: It's called birth. You don't have more than a few years left. No one does! So be happy now, without reason — or you never will be at all."

Soc's advice to "be happy *now*, without reason" may be the least understood teaching in *Way of the Peaceful Warrior*. Because deep down, the motivating force behind most of our seeking in the material, psychological, and spiritual domains is our natural human quest to *feel good more of the time, and feel bad less of the time*. With this level of understanding, our minds automatically translate *"being* happy" as *"feeling* happy."

If feeling happy was what Socrates had meant, he would have been suggesting the impossible. If we could feel happy by *willing* ourselves to be happy, we would simply do so in each moment and the game would be over. We'd just work ourselves into a feeling state of happiness and wander off into the sunset.

But as I've already mentioned, feelings change all the time, and they are not under the control of our wills. We may, in random moments, think about something pleasant and feel a little giddy, but the giddiness passes soon enough. And if we're in a funk because we just got laid off work or went bankrupt or ended a relationship, willing ourselves to feel happy isn't likely to succeed.

As you now understand, Socrates was recommending that

we act happy, because that is something we can control. We can will ourselves to smile; we can behave and move and breathe as if we're happy. Whatever the shifting state of our actual emotions, we can let our feelings be, get on with life, radiate energy into the world, and expand into the moment. This practice can be extremely difficult at times, but it remains possible. That's what Soc advised me to do, and that's what I recommend — and what I live to the best of my ability, moment to moment.

But isn't it mere pretense to act happy even if we're not feeling that way? Yes, it is — the way a terrified young soldier *pretends* to be courageous as he picks up his friend and carries him back through the firefight, the way the shy young girl walks across the middle-school dance floor and *pretends* to be confident while she asks someone to dance.

I don't care if people feel brave or energetic or confident or grateful or compassionate or kind or loving; I care whether they *act* that way. This is why Socrates recommended *unreasonable* happiness. And so do I.

What Is Enlightenment?

"Enlightenment is not an attainment, Dan; it is a Realization. And when you wake up, everything changes and nothing changes. If a blind man realizes that he can see, has the world changed?" . . .

"First mountains are mountains and rivers are rivers. Then mountains are no longer mountains and rivers are no longer rivers. Finally, mountains are mountains and rivers are rivers."

Many of us have heard or read stories about sudden and dramatic enlightenment, as if a light switch had been flicked on. I would suggest enlightenment is more often like a dimmer switch gradually being turned up, then down, then up — two steps forward, one step back. And over time, more light infuses our hearts and minds.

After enlightenment, we still need to take out the trash and do the laundry. And as the spiritual teacher Ram Dass once said, "We can be floating in cosmic bliss and still be responsible for remembering our postal code." The parade of feelings and thoughts and human relations continues, but with a different vision of the world, and that makes all the difference.

When I was trying to pin Socrates down on a definition of enlightenment, he said, "Here's one: Imagine alternating between the heights of bliss and the depths of sorrow at the speed of light." Then he walked away. His back was turned, but I suspect he had a smile on his face.

In moments of illumination, problems still exist, but we have a different relationship to them; they're no longer the foreground of our lives, only natural challenges, like fallen trees on the mountain path; as we climb over them, we sniff the air, breathe deeply, and notice the sunlight shimmering in the leaves. Our attention has risen to see beauty where before we saw only the swirling contents of our own mind. We now find blessings in small acts of kindness, and make the best of this life, this world, in whatever circumstance we find ourselves. Our eyes are focused on the bigger picture; our heads are in the clouds and our feet on solid ground. This moment may be all there is. But this moment is enough.

The Last Key on the Ring

It seemed a waste — all eight years. So here I sat on the steps, gazing over the city to the mountains beyond. Suddenly my attention

*narrowed, and the mountains began to take on a soft glow. In that
instant, I knew what I would do.*

As the English proverb goes, "Sometimes the last key on the
ring opens the door." I had to keep reminding myself of this
principle during my long quest. Socrates understood the paradox: I needed to search in order to discover what was within
me all the time — to exhaust the alternatives before I could see
the obvious. When we travel in a great circle only to return to the
point where we began, we may end up in the same place, but
with a difference: We have made the journey and explored the
periphery of the circle.

One thing about hitting emotional bottom is that we can
only go up from there. Sometimes we have to deal with the
darkness before we can see the light. So I sat on that step, feeling as if I had nowhere else to go and nothing else to do, and just
gazed at the mountains. Then, all at once, my sight cleared and
I knew. And it felt as if all my travels had only prepared me for
that moment.

Many of us have gone to bed troubled, uncertain, confused.
Then we give up, sleep, or pray on our confusion, and in the
morning a new day dawns, full of possibility, and we know what
we must do. The path may not be easy, but it's clear.

I live in a county that has one major highway that runs
north-south. That highway ascends and descends, past one hill
after another. I can't discern what's over the next hill until I
reach the peak — then it's suddenly clear. Our lives are like
those rolling hills. When everything seems hazy, it may not be
time to make decisions; we haven't yet reached the peaks of
those particular hills. It's time for patience and waiting until the
vision appears, and it will.

We make clearer decisions if we wait until we need to make them — when we reach the peaks of hills, when the time has come to act. Otherwise, it's as if we're trying to decide which of our feet we'll use to step off the curb when we're only halfway down the block.

I needed to travel around the world before I could return home with the perspective to see the next step on my path — to the mountains, and to the death and rebirth that awaited me.

ON CHAPTER EIGHT

THE GATE OPENS

Do not wait for the teachings from others,
the words of the scriptures,
the principles of enlightenment.
We are born in the morning
and we die in the evening;
the one we saw yesterday
is no longer with us today.

— BODHIN KJOLHEDE

Losing All, Gaining All

"I have nothing to bring you, Socrates. I'm still lost . . . I've failed you, and life has failed me; life has broken my heart."

*He was jubilant. "Yes! Your heart has been broken, Dan —
broken open to reveal the gate, shining within. It's the only place you haven't looked. Open your eyes . . . you've almost arrived!"*

Sometimes we have to fall to rise again — we have to surrender to triumph, let go to hold on, and allow ourselves to be broken to finally heal.

When we're insulated, protected, and comfortable, we have no incentive or reason to change, which accounts for the old proverb "God comforts the disturbed and disturbs the comfortable." And the saying "We turn to God when our foundations are shaking, only to discover that it's God who is shaking them." When life shakes us up, when we suffer great loss, we learn faith and endurance.

Reaching a dead end can bring new life, because we're forced to ask bigger questions and to look for larger truths. So, when I went to the mountains without knowing why, but trusting the impulse that I was supposed to be there, I found Socrates waiting. And what I had feared might be another dead end became a new beginning — the rebirth I had sought all those many years.

Happiness as the Way

"You've shown me the futility of searching. But isn't the way of the peaceful warrior a path, a search?" ...

"From the start, I have shown you the way of the peaceful warrior, not the way to the peaceful warrior. As long as you tread the way, you are a warrior. These past eight years you have abandoned your 'warriorship' so you could search for it. But the way is now; it always has been."

"So what do I do now? Where do I go from here?"

"Who cares?...A fool is 'happy' when his cravings are satisfied. A warrior is happy without reason. That's what makes happiness the ultimate discipline — above all else I have taught you. Happiness is not just something you feel. ...

"Feelings change, Dan. Sometimes sorrow, sometimes joy. But beneath it all remember the innate perfection of your life unfolding. That is the secret of unreasonable happiness."

I have no added commentary on this excerpt, nor is any needed. I include it here only to emphasize again one of Soc's most important teachings.

Parable of the Cave

The fire was soon crackling. Our bodies cast bizarre, twisted shadows, dancing wildly on the cave wall in front of us, as the flames consumed the logs.

Pointing to the shadows, Socrates said, "These shadows in the cave are an essential image of illusion and reality, of suffering and happiness. Here is an ancient story popularized by Plato:

"There once was a people who lived their entire lives within a Cave of Illusions. After generations, they came to believe that their own shadows, cast upon the walls, were the substance of reality. Only the myths and religious tales spoke of a brighter possibility.

"Obsessed with the shadow play, the people became accustomed to and imprisoned by their dark reality...

"Throughout history, Dan, there have been blessed exceptions to the prisoners of the Cave. There were those who became tired of the shadow play, who began to doubt it, who were no longer fulfilled by shadows no matter how high they leaped. They became seekers of light. A fortunate few found a guide who prepared them and who took them beyond all illusion into the sunlight."

The parable of the cave gives us one of the greatest metaphors of enlightenment, contrasting the dreamlike shadow play of those who still slumber with the world of sunlight and color once we step out of the cave into the light of a new reality.

It seemed appropriate for my mentor to be sharing this gift to the world from Plato, the scribe who revealed the life and teachings of the ancient Socrates. Plato's analogy of the cave has brought a measure of illumination to many generations, so that we might realize that our lives remain a shadow play — and persist in looking for the light that will lead us home.

Rebirth

The Dan Millman who had lived long ago was gone forever, a flashing moment in time — but I remained unchanged through all the ages. I was now Myself, the Consciousness that observed all, was all. All my separate parts would continue forever; forever changing, forever new.

I realized now that the Grim Reaper, the death Dan Millman had so feared, had been his great illusion. And so his life, too, had been an illusion, a problem, nothing more than a humorous incident when Consciousness had forgotten Itself.

While Dan had lived, he had not passed through the gate; he had not realized his true nature; he had lived in mortality and fear, alone.

But I knew....

I lay on the floor of the cave, smiling. I sat up and gazed into the darkness, puzzled, but without fear.

My eyes began to adjust, and I saw a white-haired man sitting nearby, smiling. Then, from thousands of years away, it all came back, and I felt momentarily saddened by my return to mortal form. Then I realized that it didn't matter — nothing could possibly matter!

This struck me as very funny; everything did, and so I started to laugh.

This was my ecstatic testimony after an ego-death vision and rebirth. Like others who have died and come back on the operating table with a new vision of life and death, I understood with certainty the illusory nature of the Dan Millman character I had been so attached to all those years. I have not taken "Dan" as seriously ever since, or felt called upon to defend his self-image.

I had finally *realized* that the awareness that was "I" did indeed animate that bodymind called Dan, but that the true "I" was infinite. In that realization, I found immortality, even as I realized that "Dan Millman" would soon vanish in a snap of eternity's fingers.

This transcendent vision has no practical value in the everyday world. It doesn't make us rich in money, only in spirit. It doesn't grant special powers like levitation, only brings more levity. We don't read others' minds, but we better understand the illusory nature of our own.

Years later, as America was reeling from the attack on September 11, 2001, I called a friend, mentor, and colleague in spirit and asked if he had any comments.

"Yes," he answered. "I'm going out to mow the lawn; the grass is still growing."

We still need to "mow the lawn," to take care of the ordinary tasks of everyday life. But as the play continues, instead of being locked into only one of our roles, we find ourselves up in the balcony at times, enjoying the show.

Awakening from the Dream

All these years Dan Millman had grown up, struggling to "be a somebody.". . .

Now I am playing Dan Millman again, and I might as well get used to it for a few more seconds in eternity, until this, too, passes. But now I know that I am not only the single piece of flesh — and that secret makes all the difference!

There was no way to describe the impact of this knowledge. I was simply awake.

*And so I awoke to reality, free of any meaning or any search.
What could there possibly be to search for? All of Soc's words had
come alive with my death. This was the paradox of it all, the humor
of it all, and the great change. All searches, all achievements, all
goals, were equally enjoyable, and equally unnecessary.*

*Energy coursed through my body. I overflowed with happiness
and burst with laughter; it was the laugh of an unreasonably happy
man. . . .*

*I had lost my mind and fallen into my heart. The gate had fi-
nally opened, and I had tumbled through, laughing, because it, too,
was . . . a gateless gate, another illusion. . . . The path would continue, without end; but now it was full of light.*

As I reread this excerpt, one of the last from *Way of the Peaceful Warrior*, I'm tempted, once again to refrain from any comment, leaving only emptiness, an expansive Zen space on the
page — because what more can I add?

It took many hours of contemplation and rewriting for me
to be able to express just the right flavor of that illumination.
The experience didn't take place in the high Sierras. But the
falling and rising, the years of searching, and the death and rebirth did indeed occur, and they set in motion all of the words
that have followed. They continue to pour from me, because
words are what I have to give.

To again quote one of my early inspirations, Ram Dass, "If
I was a singer, I would sing you a song; if I was an artist, I would
paint a picture for you. But words are what I offer." And if my
words, describing that experience, have touched something inside of you that knows, that remembers, that understands, then
I am satisfied.

Since that event, I have no longer searched for my own

sake, but rather to find new ways to extend the right leverage, at the right place, at the right time — to be of service.

Personal enlightenment affects a single drop of rain falling into the sea. But since raindrop and sea are one and the same, our collective awakening seems a quest worthy of one lifetime or many. So I continue to write and to share.

The Paradox of Experience

"You'll lose it, you know."

"Lose what?"

"Your vision. It is rare . . . but it is an experience, so you'll lose it."

"Perhaps that's true, Socrates, but who cares?" . . .

"It appears that my work with you is complete. My debt is paid."

"Do you mean this is graduation day for me?"

"No, this is graduation day for me."

Any experience passes. The intensity of the realization, the profundity and depth that had pierced me to the core, became a fond memory to draw upon — wisdom to review, like rereading a book.

Sometimes I forget; then I remember; then I forget. Moments of waking, moments of slumber. I still stumble on occasion due to lack of attention, and experience moments of irritation when I believe I know how the world should unfold. Perhaps the same is true of you.

As it turns out, as has always been the case, we have much in common. I'm very much like you because I *am* you. We're in this together. This is not mere poetry (or even particularly good prose), but it is truth. Because of our common ground, I have touched your life. Because we're not separate, you have touched mine. In the end, our stories merge, and it's graduation day for us all.

Service Call

"You will write and you will teach. You will live an ordinary life, learning how to remain ordinary in a troubled world to which, in a sense, you no longer belong. Remain ordinary, and you can be useful to others."

Way of the Peaceful Warrior was born out of my desire to share. Moved by that initial impulse, I gathered insights from explorations into the nature of mind, reality, life. Any talent I've shown for expression developed from that original passion and from the life experiences that followed. Because of my commitment to learn for the sake of others, I believe I was opened and directed to higher sources of wisdom than might have appeared had I sought to learn only for my own sake.

I'm now the teacher that Socrates once predicted. But I don't wear robes, or sit waiting on a mountaintop. I travel the city streets and country roads, passing through lives like a gentle wind, leaving whispers behind. I'm not set apart from you, for in truth I'm nothing more than your own heart speaking.

ON THE EPILOGUE
LAUGHTER IN THE WIND

Since everything is an apparition,
perfectly being what it is,
having nothing to do with good or bad,
acceptance or rejection,
one may well burst out into laughter.

— LONG CHEN PA

Wake-Up Calls in a Sleeping World

I was still living an ordinary human life with human responsibilities. I would have to adapt myself to living constructively in a world that was offended by one who is no longer interested in any search or problem. An unreasonably happy man, I learned, can grate on people's nerves!

Life is theater. We have all expressed gratitude for a gift or sorrow at someone's loss as courtesies, whether or not we were actually feeling that way. We behave with empathy and grace, playing roles appropriate to the situations in which we find ourselves.

Life involves pretense. For some, that pretense is self-serving, aimed toward gaining something; for others, it stems from kindness and consideration of the feelings and circumstances of our companions.

As we come to a point of equanimity with the play of light and shadow in the world around us, we learn, in the words of mythologist and writer Joseph Campbell, "to go with joy among the sorrows of the world." To some people this statement may seem callous, but what's our alternative? A long face will not heal the world. To live with joy in this world is an act of courage.

I've learned the wisdom of behaving with kindness and compassion whether or not I feel that way. I've learned to say "Thank you!" whether or not I feel grateful. Likewise, we can behave with a relaxed confidence even when we're feeling shy, or with courage even when we're afraid.

And here again is another of Soc's great secrets: We can behave in an enlightened manner whether or not we feel enlightened. To do so is a sacred act, but an act just the same. This divine pretense is what the years have taught me, and it requires all that is within us. This was Soc's way, the way of the peaceful warrior.

The Teacher Is Everywhere

Before walking back to my wife, my home, my friends, and my future, I surveyed the world around me. Socrates was here. He was everywhere.

Many devoted readers have expressed a kind of sorrow that they don't have a teacher like Socrates in their lives. They have not yet understood that I wrote *Way of the Peaceful Warrior* to share him freely.

We have all heard the saying "When the student is ready, the teacher appears." The point of the ending of *Way of the Peaceful Warrior* is that when the student is ready, the teacher appears *everywhere*. Look to the mountains, the streams, the changing seasons and tides. Look to the people and relationships in your life. They all reveal the secret of life. But are you paying attention? Are you open enough to see it, to feel it, to realize the perfect truth of this moment?

If so, there's nothing else to do but open your arms and your heart and welcome each passing moment. If this simple truth is not yet alive in you, stay with it, act as if it is, and be gentle with yourself along the way.

CONCLUSION TO
THE COMMENTARIES

Give us rain when we expect sun;
Give us music when we expect trouble;
Give us tears when we expect breakfast;
Give us dreams when we expect a storm;
Give us a stray dog when we expect congratulations.
Dear God, play with us,
Turn us sideways, and around.

— ANONYMOUS PRAYER

So now we have made another journey through *Way of the Peaceful Warrior.* I was once the sole protagonist of my story, the reluctant hero making his passage through the shadow lands, with Socrates as my mentor and guide. But now my teacher has become yours.

We are each protagonists of our own stories in the making, with many chapters left to write. Wherever your story leads, keep your eyes and heart open. I hope these commentaries have shed new light on the way. As you continue up the mountain path, I wish you good journeys.

ACKNOWLEDGMENTS

*We are all looking for someone
who will make us do what we can.*

— RALPH WALDO EMERSON

My gratitude to the "usual suspects" in my literary posse, support system, and safety net: Linda Kramer of H J Kramer Inc, who took on the project with gusto and who sent the first check; the capable and dedicated staff at New World Library, who do everything else — Munro Magruder, Georgia Hughes, Tona Pearce Myers, Mary Ann Casler, Monique Muhlenkamp, and the rest of the team.

Nancy Grimley Carleton served as primary editor; Jason Gardner and Kristen Cashman at New World provided additional insights and polish.

Special thanks to Ruby Yeh, who produced an earlier and still-popular multimedia eBook titled *The Peaceful Warrior E-Xperience*, based upon material in this volume. Her energy and immediacy helped get the entire project moving.

As always, my beloved wife, Joy, continues to serve as muse, guardian angel, and source of wisdom, support, and inspiration.

Thanks also to Michael Larsen and Elizabeth Pomada, founders of the San Francisco Writers Conference, who originally placed *Way of the Peaceful Warrior* many years ago — and to Jeremy Tarcher, who first published it.

And, finally, deepest gratitude to my longtime publisher, visionary artist, and respected friend Hal Kramer, whose faith brought the book back to life in 1984. Hal, you helped to change many lives.

A CHRONOLOGY OF BOOKS

*A house without books
is like a room without windows.*

— HORACE MANN

The first book I wrote, *Way of the Peaceful Warrior*, managed to capture a young protagonist's transformation from living a conventional life to embodying transcendent vision in a way that many readers could relate to.

During the writing, several chapters about physical training interfered with the story narration, so I pulled them out. Soon after, those chapters took on a life of their own and became my first published book (in 1979) about training body, mind, and spirit. It was titled *Whole Body Fitness* — a work that sold modestly before quietly going out of print.

In 1980, when my first book "died," my second one was

born. *Way of the Peaceful Warrior* came out in hardcover, found its way into a few bookstores, and then, like my first book, died young. However, in 1984 a retired publisher, Hal Kramer, read an old copy and decided to republish it. So *Way of the Peaceful Warrior* was born again and picked up momentum from there.

Soon after, in 1985, another small publisher republished my physical training book under the title *The Warrior Athlete*. In 1996, it came out under a third title, *The Inner Athlete*, and in 1999 found its final form as *Body Mind Mastery*.

After writing *Way of the Peaceful Warrior* in 1980, I didn't write another book for ten years, because I had nothing new to say (a fact I hope some readers find refreshing). But then came new experiences, travels, mentors, and masters — a true story I will relate in a forthcoming book, *My Search for Spirit*.

In 1990, I wrote an adventure, *Sacred Journey of the Peaceful Warrior*. The events I relate in *Sacred Journey* occurred not after, but rather within, the original story. In other words, someone who hasn't read either book might want to read *Way of the Peaceful Warrior* to the point where my travels begin — and then read *Sacred Journey* before finishing *Way of the Peaceful Warrior*. It's not necessary to read the books in that order, but it makes the most sense in terms of chronology.

I had no plans to write additional books, but many readers of the first two *Peaceful Warrior* volumes wrote saying, "I was inspired by your first two books, but how do you apply all that information to everyday life?" In response, I wrote *No Ordinary Moments* to clarify all I had learned up to that time. It would be the first in a series of nonfiction guidebooks that have come to offer a comprehensive course in what I call "the peaceful warrior's way" — practical wisdom for living with peaceful hearts and warrior spirits as we evolve in the school of everyday life.

If you want to understand the power and beauty of the three

selves or the tower of seven levels (how awareness rises up through the chakras), you'll want to read *Sacred Journey*.

If you'd like to learn more about the term *peaceful warrior* or the arena of daily life, or what to do when the going gets tough, then read *No Ordinary Moments*, which also contains information about universal addictions and how to manage them, as well as material on the will to change and the power of happiness.

If you have youngsters, they might enjoy two children's books I wrote in the early 1990s, when my children were still immersed in the magical world of picture books: *Secret of the Peaceful Warrior* and *Quest for the Crystal Castle* — beautifully illustrated by T. Taylor Bruce, with positive lessons about courage and kindness.

If you seek clarity about your life purpose — the core issues, obstacles, and strengths on your path (and those of your parents, children, friends, and loved ones) — and also wish to learn how to overcome the inner obstacles you were born to conquer, you'll find much of interest in *The Life You Were Born to Live*.

To understand the twelve spiritual laws that can enrich and facilitate every aspect of your life, you can travel in the mountains with me and an ageless woman sage in *The Laws of Spirit*.

If you're ready to face the gauntlet of the twelve gateways to spiritual growth and the liberation of attention, you can find a good map in my most comprehensive guidebook, *Everyday Enlightenment*.

If you'd like to better understand and utilize the House Rules that Socrates referred to in *Way of the Peaceful Warrior*, you'll find twenty-four of these universal laws, as well as commentary on their application, in one of my most reader-friendly books, *Living on Purpose*.

If you enjoy inspiring stories of mystery and miracles that changed lives, you'll find many in *Divine Interventions*, which I wrote with my friend Doug Childers.

Twenty years after writing *Way of the Peaceful Warrior*, in response to readers' queries about Socrates — including questions about whether he was married or had children, and about his teachers and the experiences that tempered his spirit and developed his power and wisdom — I wrote the story of his life in *The Journeys of Socrates*, about the value of family and a quest for salvation. It describes how a boy became a man, how a man became a warrior, and how a warrior found peace.

And finally, in 2006, when the *Peaceful Warrior* movie opened across America, the time had come to write *Wisdom of the Peaceful Warrior* in order to clarify the substance of my first book, a quarter century after I first wrote it.

My next book will be titled *My Search for Spirit*. This entirely factual account will tell the story behind the peaceful warrior saga, relating my adventures and lessons with four other mentors who helped shape my life and work — adventures that reflect our hearts' deepest longings and our shared spiritual quest.

ABOUT THE AUTHOR

 Dan Millman is a former world-champion gymnast, university coach, martial arts instructor, and college professor. His numerous books have inspired millions of readers in more than thirty languages.

His talks and workshops in the United States and abroad, presenting practical ways to live with a peaceful heart and a warrior's spirit, have influenced leaders in the fields of health, psychology, education, business, sports, and the arts.

Married for thirty years, Dan has three grown daughters — and two grandchildren so far.

To contact Dan's office, join his eList,
or receive information about his books, DVDs,
audios, speaking schedule, and more, visit:

www.peacefulwarrior.com

H J Kramer and New World Library are dedicated to
publishing books and audio products
that inspire and challenge us to improve
the quality of our lives and our world.

Our products are available
in bookstores everywhere.
For our catalog, please contact:

New World Library
14 Pamaron Way
Novato, California 94949

Phone: (415) 884-2100 or (800) 972-6657
Catalog requests: Ext. 50
Orders: Ext. 52
Fax: (415) 884-2199

E-mail: escort@newworldlibrary.com
Website: www.newworldlibrary.com